Believing by Emotions

Believing BY Emotions

ACHIEVE THE IMPOSSIBLE BY RECEIVING MORE HELP FROM YOUR HIGHER POWER

BOB RAYBOULD

Believing BY Emotions
PUBLISHING

Believing BY Emotions
PUBLISHING

Believing by Emotions
Copyright © 2025 by Bob Raybould

All rights reserved. No part of this publication may be reproduced, distributed, or transmitted in any form or by any means, including photocopying, recording, or other electronic or mechanical methods, without the prior written permission of the copyright holder, except in the case of brief quotations embodied in critical reviews and certain other noncommercial uses permitted by copyright law.

Hardcover ISBN: 979-8-218-65054-4
Paperback ISBN: 979-8-218-65053-7

To the patience of my wife, Nancy, and my family as I have exposed and eliminated (and continue to expose and eliminate) my many false ideas. To my many editors who have helped me understand these laws of nature well enough to write a book about them. With especial thanks to my final editor, Anna Krusinski. To those who were able to use these laws before I fully understood them. And, finally, to all who have listened to me as I have tried to articulate my growing understanding of these laws.

Also, to my friend Johnnie Bryant, who is willing to recommend this book based on his successful use of these principles many years ago before I fully understood them.

Contents

Introduction..ix
One: More Truth, More Success 1
Two: More Success, More Happiness...........35
Three: The Power of the Future with BBE..................57
Four: Using BBE..65
Five: Ideas That Will Help You Succeed.....................95
Six: Using BBE to Become a Better Person 105
Seven: Gaining More Peace 117
Eight: Sharing the Bounty...137
Final Comments..149
About the Author..153
Blank BBE Sheets..157

Introduction

CAN YOU AFFORD TO TAKE the time to read this book?

I believe you can. *Believing by Emotions* introduces a new application of age-old principles that will enable you to increase your happiness, strengthen your belief and faith, boost your self-esteem, and improve faster in every area of your life.

If you take the time to read this book, you will learn about Believing by Emotions (BBE), a tool based on laws of nature that will enable you to have more happiness in your life and accomplish twice as much per unit of time (minutes, hours, days, weeks, months, or years) spent. It is not as revolutionary as the discovery of the wheel, but it will feel equally remarkable once you start seeing the results in your own life.

BELIEVING BY EMOTIONS

If you want to be happier and accomplish more in the future, then I believe you will be wise to take the time to read this book now. And if you want to increase your faith in your higher power and in yourself—and become a better person—I encourage you to start using the tool right away. Whether you just read the book or actually use the tool, I promise you the effort will be worth it.

Just reading the book will not be enough to gain all the benefits of this tool, but it will give you the understanding that this wonderful tool exists and is always available for you to use. I have introduced BBE to hundreds of people, and many have missed out on its power because they were not willing to do the hard work necessary to see results. For them, it was just another good idea they assumed they already knew about. It is not just another idea; it is a totally different way to move forward and achieve results. Others have brushed it off because they were "too busy" to learn something new that would enable them to be happier and reach their objectives in less than half the time. It is OK to not work on using the tool right away. In the beginning, I just want you to understand BBE well enough to know that you have this resource when the time comes that you will want to use it.

If you do take the time to start using BBE on a small goal, this will help you understand the tool at the experiential level. And when you eventually use it on a bigger goal, you will be able to do everything faster and more easily. But the biggest benefit you'll receive from using

INTRODUCTION

the tool will be the happiness you'll experience during the journey.

I know this to be true. I have used BBE for over fifty years. I have also seen others gain increased happiness and make significant changes in their lives. This tool has enabled me to dramatically deepen my faith in my higher power, do more of the actions I know will benefit my life, increase my income, rapidly gain financial independence, love myself as I am, love others as they are, love my higher power more fully, understand that my higher power comprehends more than I can comprehend, achieve objectives that I would have never thought possible, improve my relationships, and become a far better person than I was before. And it has enabled me to have each of these growth journeys in an easy, rapid, and pleasant way. BBE will do this for you, too, because it is based on natural laws that always work.

Throughout my five decades of experience as an accomplished salesman and businessman, my key to successful investing has been my ability to recognize when the normal "risk relationship" is heavily in the favor of my investors. As a result, my investors' returns were about twice the normal returns for similar investments. All investments have risk, and all offer rewards. In most cases, if the potential for reward is high, then the risk is also higher than normal. Conversely, if the potential for reward is low (like in a federally insured bank's savings account), then the level of risk is much lower than normal. If you can find an investment that offers a high reward (similar to or better than that offered by the stock market) with a level of risk below that of a bank savings account, this is a great investment. Warren Buffett, the best investor of our time, calls these types of investments "no-brainers."

BBE is, in my opinion, a no-brainer. The risk is that you might spend some time reading this short book. In exchange, you will discover a totally new approach to personal and spiritual growth. When you want to move forward in your life, this tool will enable you to work through the four-step process that will provide you with more happiness, improve your self-view, and supercharge your actions and results. You will be well rewarded for your time. This is the best no-brainer you will ever come across.

The laws on which BBE is based are natural laws that always work. It is a near certainty that BBE will work for you. You will be happier, and you will have achieved your goal. Plus, the hours spent will have saved you weeks (if not months) of effort in the future. Achieving goals in half the time will make many impossible goals now possible.

Are you ready to invest in the beautiful life and unlimited potential that is waiting for you?

—Bob Raybould

ONE

More Truth, More Success

BELIEVING BY EMOTIONS (BBE) IS a tool for personal growth and rapidly gaining more happiness, and it is based on three laws of nature; these are absolute truths, and they never fail.

The first two natural laws upon which this tool is based are accepted by all. First, that we are each born unique, and during our lives, we gain our own set of truths and limiting false ideas. Second, that the more truth we have in our lives, the better our lives work and the happier we are.

Now, the third natural law may be new to you—and it holds the key to gaining more happiness, strengthening your faith, and experiencing more success in your life. This third law is that, by accumulating enough emotions, we can receive help from our higher power to assist us in removing our limiting false ideas and replacing them with more truth.

BBE integrates these three laws of nature to create a path to happiness and success that is faster, easier, and more enjoyable than anything you've ever tried before.

> If you're like me, and you don't like to read—if you like to get to the nuggets of truth without going through all of the words—you can skip to chapter 4 and start using BBE right away. This tool is enormously powerful, but you do not need to read the whole book to gain its value; the real value will come as you use the tool.
>
> So, to get started now, think of a small goal in one area of your life where you want to expand your faith, gain more happiness, and have a more positive view of yourself. It should be something you know you can accomplish in a few days or weeks but just have not done yet. Then, read chapter 4 and start using BBE. After you've achieved your first goal and have experienced the power of BBE, you can then return to the beginning of the book to deepen your understanding of the tool and learn how to achieve bigger goals—and do it faster and more easily. Enjoy!

Each of us are spirit children of our higher power; we were born innocent and complete. Before we came to earth, we were first created spiritually by our higher power. We were then born with the innate ability to feel contentment and peace, and we were inherently able to give and receive love. We were born with the unique DNA, talents, abilities, and potential we needed to succeed.

Then, as we grew older, our experiences caused us to accumulate false ideas about ourselves. But these are just a small portion of our total package of false ideas. We also carry with us all of our ancestors' false ideas. They all made mistakes and accumulated their own false ideas, which caused them to have an inaccurate view of themselves. They then passed those down to their children and grandchildren—and ultimately, to us. The same is true for everyone we've associated with. Just like us, they have had huge amounts of false ideas passed down to them. And, in turn, they have passed some of their false ideas to us. As a result, we each end up with more false ideas than we can ever understand. We do not know where they came from or when we got them. But they are there. When we attempt to do something, they hold us back. Why? Because we are wired to act in harmony with the way we see ourselves. These false ideas have blinded us from seeing the potential that has been imbued in us from our higher power. This gives our false ideas control over the way we act, and the way we view our lives and the world around us. All of this holds us back from fully connecting with our higher power and reaching our full potential.

In my case, I was born into a situation that provided me with unique advantages and unique disadvantages. As my life played out, all these combined and I learned a unique set of beliefs. Some of these beliefs were true and helped me move forward, and some were false—and these false beliefs kept me from seeing who I truly was; that I was born with all the abilities and talents I needed to be happy and succeed. I was still that person, but my false ideas were keeping me from seeing who I really was.

I had dyslexia and spent two years in the second grade. My father's experience in World War I left him with mental problems that he treated with alcohol. My mother's life was difficult and caused her to not feel or show emotions. Our family finances were relatively good, but also unstable. All these and other factors caused me to gain many false ideas about myself.

I struggled in school, but I found a way to succeed. I had both failures and successes, but my determination kept me moving forward in life. As the years passed, I faced more challenges, and the false ideas that I had accumulated caused me to go in circles instead of solving them. Then (as I will explain later), in my late twenties, I had a big failure. But, with persistence, I kept trying to succeed.

Up to that point, my life had been made up of a constant series of successes and failures, and my life looked like this:

Then, at the suggestion of a book I was reading to help me succeed, I listened to a recording called "The Strangest Secret" by the radio speaker and author, Earl Nightingale. Recorded in 1953, it was first given as a presentation to a group of salesmen and is now available on YouTube. The main message is that our thoughts shape who we become. (Many of Nightingale's examples are male-oriented, but women can gain value from the recording as well, if they can overlook this fact.) I listened to the recording repeatedly, and it opened my mind to thinking differently; I began to see that I could change my life by changing my thoughts. I also realized that I had more ability than I was showing in my actions, and if I didn't change my thoughts and actions, I would remain stuck—as I was and where I was. Before listening to "The Strangest Secret," I had been addicted to thinking and acting like a person who failed often. But, after listening to it many times, I came to believe that, if I could learn to think differently, I could also more easily act differently and change my results.

This new realization led me to discover a self-improvement method which I called Believing by Emotions, or BBE. By using BBE, I was able to accumulate enough positive emotions to gain true ideas that replaced my false ideas concerning myself as a businessman. Once my self-view changed and I saw myself as a successful businessman, my higher power was then free to help me. You see, our higher power will never force us to grow or change. But, when we adjust our self-view and come

BELIEVING BY EMOTIONS

to know that we are capable of succeeding, we enable our higher power to give us more assistance. So, when I started using BBE to align my self-view with the goal I wanted to achieve, I also opened my heart to receiving assistance from my higher power. As a result, I went on to success after success in business. From then on, my life in business looked like this:

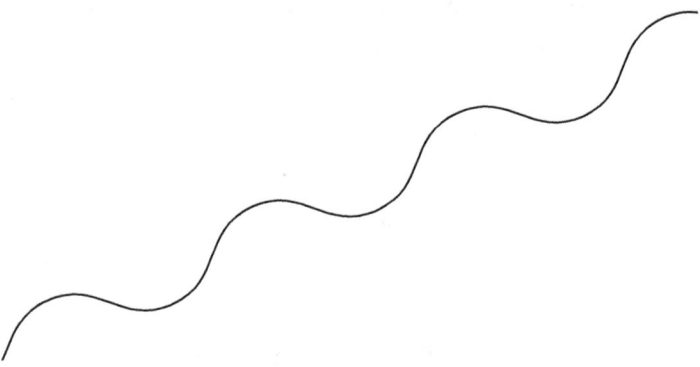

These two lines tell part of my story. The second line (after using BBE to achieve success) is about half as long as the first line (when I was still struggling before discovering BBE). Not only did I succeed, but I did it in about half the time it would have taken if I had continued to use traditional methods for growth and change. In addition, my journey forward was much more happy and joyful.

BBE is an entirely different approach from traditional methods of self-improvement. With traditional methods, we set a goal, and then we fight through our accumulated lies and false ideas while we try to achieve our goal. Throughout this process, our self-view is that of a person who has not yet succeeded, and so our minds are working to keep us where we are.

With BBE, we set a goal, and then we accumulate positive emotions to change the way we see ourselves and eliminate our false ideas *before* we work on achieving our goal.

> **How to Accumulate Emotions**
>
> BBE is totally different from anything you've ever tried before, and it's so easy to do—once you know how to accumulate emotions. In chapter 4, you'll learn the four steps to follow to use BBE. But for now, you might be wondering what it means to accumulate emotions.
>
> It's as simple as identifying four emotions you'll be feeling in the weeks or months after you've achieved your goal, and then repeating those emotions to yourself over and over again until you feel them deeply. You can choose to cycle through your four emotions quickly (I can go through mine about ten times in a minute), or you can sit with each emotion for a minute or more. That's all there is to it!

Now our minds are helping us act in the way we see ourselves, as someone who is already successful in the area of our goal. This enables us to receive assistance from our higher power, the source of absolute truth. And the more we do this, the more we put ourselves in a position to receive more guidance and help. This is what makes the tool so powerful. With this process, we are happy during the entire journey. In addition, because BBE enables us to free ourselves from our false ideas before we begin—when we are rested and fresh—the process is much easier and faster. If, in the process of learning to use BBE, you also spend two to three hours listening to "The Strangest Secret," the combination of the two will save you days, weeks, and even years of effort in the future.

BBE is such a different approach, and I never would have discovered it without first repeatedly listening to "The Strangest Secret." I am grateful that Earl Nightingale was able to share his special insights with us. I have simply added to his wonderful guidance with the process of feeling emotions. The recording not only taught me the additional truths I needed to learn before I could succeed; it also helped me overcome my addiction to thinking like someone who often failed.

Because I know firsthand the profound impact of listening to "The Strangest Secret" along with using BBE, I recommend that you start there. By listening to the recording a few times, you will come to know that you can shape your success by changing the way you think about yourself. Then, by using BBE, you'll take that one step further by accumulating emotions so that you can start thinking differently and change how you see yourself. This will bring you happiness, help from your own mind, and assistance from your higher power. I have introduced BBE to many people, but those who first repeatedly listened to the recording have been the most successful in using this tool.

A Brief Overview of Believing by Emotions

Believing by Emotions (BBE) is a tool that has been of enormous help to me. If you choose to use it, your life will improve far beyond your expectations. And the additional goals that you will be able to achieve will open your understanding to more of your true potential.

With BBE, you will learn to accumulate enough positive emotions to change the way you see yourself. This will expose your negative false ideas about yourself. Once you know they are false, your mind will eliminate them. The more false ideas you remove, the happier you will be, and the more you will reconnect with your true self and see yourself as the winner you were when you were born. You will then do whatever it takes to reach your goals. Because you will have replaced your false ideas with truth, you will find it easy to act like this person would act and create the results this person would create. This will enable you to gain more help from your higher power, which has all knowledge and wants the best for you. This assistance will be in harmony with the way you see yourself. Your higher power will not have to force you to improve, because you will already see yourself that way; your higher power will simply be free to assist you in doing what you already know you can do.

Going through this process will also enable you to better serve and love others. As you do this, you will also love yourself more. And the more you conform your life to what you believe your higher power is teaching you, the better your life will work. This will open the door to receiving even more help and blessings from your higher power. These are the great gifts of using BBE. As you use it, you will bring benefits to yourself and to others. The more truth you have, the more love will motivate your actions. It is all about love. More love will make your journey full of joy and happiness.

I discovered BBE in 1968, when I was on the verge of a huge failure. I was so desperate that I was willing to try anything. In doing that, I discovered this amazing tool.

At the age of thirty-two, I was married to a wonderful woman, had two wonderful children, and had served successfully in the United States Army in Germany for two years. I had just resigned from a position with a large corporation in New York, and I was returning to Salt Lake City, Utah, to sell life insurance. I had been an insurance salesman three years earlier, and at that time, I had not been successful. I had given up and had used my MBA to gain the job in New York. This time, I was desperate to succeed.

But, instead of succeeding, I was doing as I had been doing three years earlier. I saw myself as someone who would not succeed, and my mind was making sure I produced those kinds of results. I was constantly asking for help. My higher power wanted to help me, but in doing so, my higher power would have been forcing me to succeed. That would have violated my freedom to choose.

And so I was going forward and backward, not making any real progress. I was having ups and downs, and I was stuck at the same low level of personal acceptance.

Then, I discovered BBE, and my business life changed. In the process of applying BBE to my work, I went on to incredible success and my feelings about myself greatly improved. I still had struggles and setbacks along the way, but I was able to quickly overcome them and continue to move forward. Because my mind was helping me instead of holding me back, I was able to succeed in a fraction of the time. And the help I received from my higher power made possible levels of success and happiness far beyond my expectations. When I first discovered BBE, I attempted to share it with others because I was so amazed by the change it had made in my life. Fast-forward more than five decades, and I am still committed to sharing the power of BBE, which is why I have spent the last five years drafting this book (and my other book, *Success by Emotions*) so I can share this tool with anyone who is willing to use it.

BBE will challenge you to think differently about yourself and see yourself in a new way. It takes courage to do something different and new. Thinking differently is hard (if not impossible) unless we first have a desire and prepare ourselves to do so. A strong desire may be enough for some. But it was not enough for me. I needed to repeatedly listen to "The Strangest Secret" to prepare myself for the process of using BBE.

BELIEVING BY EMOTIONS

Many of us are comfortable with the way we are, even if we want to do more or be more. We shy away from change because it can feel overwhelming. But BBE is entirely different from anything you have used to change. The beauty of BBE is that it doesn't require you to change who you are; you already have everything you need to succeed, you just need to reconnect with that truth. BBE helps you more accurately see your full potential that was given to you by your higher power. And, when you do, it becomes easy—and even enjoyable—to think differently, act differently, and change your life for the better. And listening to "The Strangest Secret" will help you overcome your habits of thinking the way you now think, so that you can be ready to use BBE.

Rather than listening to the recording, you may be able to jump in and start using BBE right away, but I have seen time and again that those who have achieved the greatest results from using BBE started by learning additional truth from the recording and changing their habit of thinking in their old, negative ways.

Throughout the rest of this chapter, I will explain how BBE works. Then, with that understanding, you can decide if you want to try the rapid approach, or if you want to take time and first listen to "The Strangest Secret." The latter approach will take longer, but if you take the time to listen to the recording, I can almost guarantee that you will have greater success using BBE.

Why Is Change So Difficult?

We all fight against growth and change, even when we know that it will benefit us. So what keeps us stuck?

1. **We're taught to conform.** As we go to school and live our lives, we are taught to follow the rules and learn the proper ways to behave. We are taught that conformity is the path to success. But, as my son has taught me, any idea taken too far can cause problems. We also develop a strong desire to conform our lives to the way we are currently thinking. We want to stay the way we are, and we become almost addicted to thinking the way we have always thought. But this limits our creativity. A wise man once told me years ago that "if nothing changes, everything remains the same." Conforming keeps everything from changing. But we know that more truth will make our lives better, and using BBE requires that we let go of our false ideas and replace them with truth. This requires change.

2. **We fear the unknown.** What will our lives be like after we change? We can't predict the future, but what we do know is that life does not stand still. We can either continue to gain more false ideas, or we can change our lives and accumulate more truth. Using BBE can provide peace of mind in knowing that, although our lives will be different afterward, they will also be *better*.

3. **Our false ideas are powerful.** The limiting beliefs we've accumulated have been in control for a long time. Sometimes, it can even seem like they've defined who we are. But the truth is that we are so much more than that, and our false ideas can only continue to exist as long as we believe in them. In using BBE, we eliminate those false ideas and gain more control, which makes it much easier to succeed.
4. **We don't have time.** Many of us think we don't have time to make changes or go after our goals. But that is not a valid excuse. Using BBE saves months (and, in some cases, years) of time by enabling us to reach our goals faster than anything we've tried before. Yes, it will take time to read this book and apply its principles. But those few hours spent will save you so much more time in the long run. And the more you use BBE, the faster you will make changes and come to see yourself as someone who has already succeeded. For example, my first enormous change took me three weeks. Now, I can make changes of similar importance in about three days.

So, while there are many reasons why it can feel hard to make changes in your life, the happiness and success you'll gain from using BBE will be well worth the effort. Achieving your first goal will feel the hardest because you will not only be removing the false ideas that are keeping you from your goal, but you will also be overcoming the false ideas that are telling you not to change. Trust in the process; BBE will make it fun and easy to reach your goals. And having a happy journey along the way will be your greatest reward.

To help you better understand what's holding you back from making the changes you want to achieve, I'd like you to imagine your mind as an iceberg. The top 30 percent of the iceberg represents the way you *want* to see yourself—what you want to achieve and what you believe you can achieve. The bottom 70 percent of the iceberg, the part that's hidden underwater, represents your false ideas about yourself. You do not know where they came from, when you got them, or why you believe them. This bottom part of the iceberg is the one in charge, and it's keeping you from being successful and happy.

You cannot see the full iceberg; just as you cannot see your true self, the version of yourself that your higher power intended you to be. However, BBE offers you a tool to gain more of this truth.

Without BBE, when you attempt to reach a goal, you are creating a conflict. The top part of the iceberg believes you can do it, and the bottom part sees you as someone who will not succeed. This causes the journey to be difficult, and you're likely to fail often. If you eventually succeed, the bottom part of the iceberg changes to reflect that success until it matches the top part of the iceberg. You now see yourself as the person you aspired to be. But this approach takes many years and can be a frustrating process.

Instead, with BBE, you first change the way you see yourself so that the bottom and the top of your iceberg see you as someone who has already succeeded. Then your mind will help you succeed because you are hardwired to act according to your self-perception. And once you believe in your own potential, you will also open yourself to receiving help from your higher power which is finally free to help you succeed. With this assistance, you will reach your goal in half the time, and you'll have so much fun doing it.

Your life is composed of many different icebergs; one for each aspect of your life. But the good news is that, once you use BBE to improve one of your icebergs or one part of your life, that positive change will stay with you. The more one area is full of truth, the happier you will be and the more successful you will become in that area of your life. In time, more of your life will be in harmony and you will increase your level of overall truth. You will believe more in your higher power, in yourself, and in the tool—and you will continue to have success and happiness in every aspect of your life.

Gaining More Truth with BBE

As I mentioned earlier, we were born with everything we needed to succeed. We had many inborn talents and abilities (we still have them; this is who we really are).

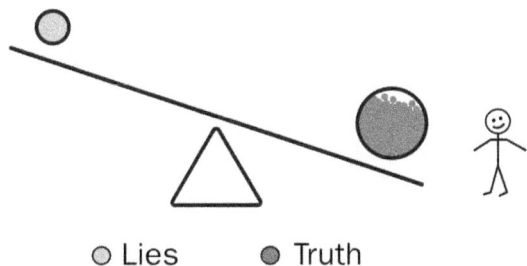

○ Lies   ● Truth

As babies, and soon afterward, it was easy for us to succeed because we saw ourselves accurately. Without great struggle, we learned to eat, walk, talk, and run. It was easy for us to develop our talents and abilities.

But then life happened. We had different experiences. During some of these experiences, we gained false ideas about ourselves and became disconnected from our innate abilities. We began to see ourselves less accurately. For example, at age three, we all could paint beautifully; we just naturally accessed the potential we were born with. Many years later, after accumulating judgments and expectations about ourselves, we've become convinced that only a lucky few are "talented enough" to paint beautifully; we've overlooked the natural potential we had accessed so easily when we were children.

BELIEVING BY EMOTIONS

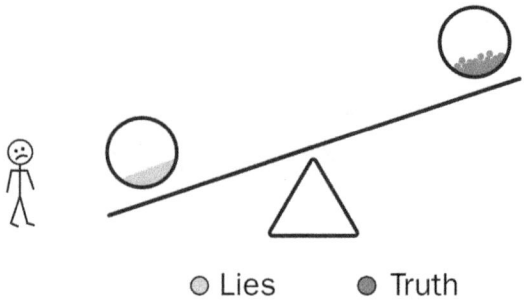

○ Lies ● Truth

These false ideas tell us that we can't do things we have the ability to do. They slow our progress, and in some cases, even stop it altogether.

We use BBE to eliminate these false ideas by accumulating positive emotions that lead us to our true selves. By doing this, we are able to see ourselves more accurately. We again see that we have the ability to succeed. This flips the scale away from our lies and false ideas, and toward the truth about who we are. And when we think more positively about ourselves, that changes how we act and what results we create. This, in turn, enables our higher power to give us whatever assistance we need to reach our goal.

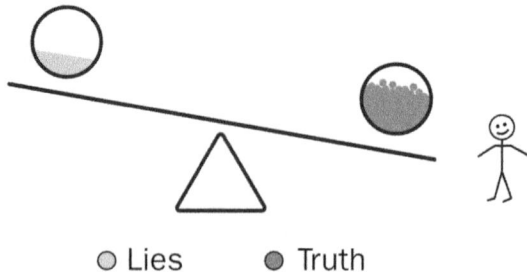

○ Lies ● Truth

BBE works because it is centered around absolute truths, and it never fails. As Dr. Russell M. Nelson, one of the early pioneers of open-heart surgery, explains in his book, *Heart of the Matter: What 100 Years of Living Have Taught Me*:

> There are absolute truths, and there are relative truths. Relative truths often change as science and discovery produce knowledge heretofore unknown. Relative truths can also change as a result of personal opinion. But absolute truths never change. Gravity is an absolute truth. Gravity never varies. [...] Absolute truths are completely reliable, even incontrovertible. They do not change. This means that procedures and practices based on divine laws will work every time.

The laws of nature always work. And the more we follow them, the better things work. Gravity always works. Planes with the proper engineering are always lifted up when they reach the necessary speed.

When Dr. Nelson was in medical school, doctors believed that, if anyone touched a human heart, it would stop. In time, they found that they could touch a heart, and it would continue beating. Then, they found they could handle a heart, and it would still continue to beat. They eventually developed a heart-lung machine so they could remove the heart from the body and the patient would continue to live. They later found that, if they altered the sodium-potassium ratio in the heart, it would stop beating, which would enable them to perform

BELIEVING BY EMOTIONS

intricate operations that would be impossible to do while the heart was moving. Then, they discovered that, when they washed the potassium out with normal blood, the heart would start beating again. The more practice they had, the more they refined how they used this law of nature. But their refinements did not change the law; the surgeons just changed their understanding of the details that made the law work. Each new discovery allowed them to progress forward in doing heart surgery, and these pioneers found that this law of nature will always work.

The more truth we have about these laws of nature, the better our lives work. And the more we use these laws, the more they can help us move forward. The laws do not change, but our new understanding of them enables us to more easily change our lives for the better.

About sixty years ago, David C. Evans (the father of my good friend, David F. Evans), woke his son in the middle of the night to tell him that he had just put the first dot on a computer screen. He had discovered how to use another law. From that first dot, we now have all the marvelous smartphones and computer graphics we have today.

Each new discovery of truth opens the door for additional discoveries. Some discoveries are made after years of research. Others, like the apple falling on Sir Issac Newton's head, happen by chance. All these discoveries are made by brilliant scientists who have spent hours learning and experimenting. I am far from being a great scientist. As you will learn later, it was by pure accident that I discovered the natural laws that make BBE work. I simply sat down in a new car, and it made me feel different.

When I read these words in Dr. Nelson's book, a light bulb went on for me:

> "Surely," I thought, "there must be laws, or truths, that govern the beating heart." If we could discover those laws and then "obey" them, the results would be positive. It was the very idea that absolute truths, or divine laws, exist—and that following them would produce desirable results—that gave me new hope about discovering ways to repair a defective heart.

I realized that BBE works based on three absolute truths. The more I could understand BBE, the more I could use those truths to help myself and others move forward in their lives. BBE works—and will always work—because it is based on laws of nature. If we accumulate enough emotions, we will open our hearts to receive help from our higher power in exposing our unique false ideas, and our lives will improve as a result. This will always be true, and our higher power will always be there to assist us.

As we discussed earlier, throughout our lives, we acquire relative truths about ourselves. They keep us from seeing the absolute truths about who we are. In using BBE, we regain those absolute truths; this changes the way we see ourselves and helps us change the way we perform and the results we accomplish. We gain a better view of who we are and what we can accomplish. Then, when our minds see that our old beliefs have been exposed as false, our minds now always treat those beliefs differently. The true ideas that replaced them are now in control, and the false beliefs are released. The longer we have held a false belief, the more emotions are keeping it in place. This means we need more emotions to expose it as false. But the natural laws that are working remain the same.

As studies are done on these principles, we will gain a clearer understanding of how these natural laws work. But, in the meantime, these laws will continue to work, and you can utilize their power with BBE.

Testimonial

"I was initially skeptical when Bob first introduced me to Believing by Emotions. I approached the process with openness and a desire to believe that it could help me, but in the back of my mind, I wondered, 'What are the odds that this little book will help me?'

"I had read so many self-help books over the years, and I'd recently become increasingly obsessed with self-improvement, and yet, I was still stuck. I felt like I was spinning my wheels and getting nowhere. I understood the concepts of manifestation, visualization, belief, and mindset, but I couldn't flip that switch to change my limiting beliefs about myself. I was making little steps of progress here and there, and

I found encouragement and insight in many of the books I was reading. But I knew I was still missing something. I was always looking for the next book, the next breakthrough, the next solution, unknowingly reaffirming to myself that I wasn't enough, that I needed some external knowledge and force to fix me. I felt lost.

"I had blocks that were keeping me from flowing. I've always been drawn to the analogy of a river. It flows effortlessly; it doesn't need help, it doesn't need anyone to get in there and push the water downstream. I've always wanted my life to flow like a river, and yet I felt the need to continually push when my flow was dammed up. I was fruitlessly trying to push through my life without first removing the blocks—the limiting beliefs, the fallen logs and debris of negative experiences and emotions that I'd allowed into my being. I was denying my natural state of flowing with ease. Like so many people, I was allowing past experiences, pains, failures, and rejections to define me. I knew this conceptually, but I still tried to push because it was all I knew how to do.

"By using BBE and switching my focus to really feeling how I wanted to be and how I would feel when I achieved my goals, those blocks have naturally begun to dissolve and break apart. All that focus I was giving to my problems was only reinforcing those blockages and damming up my river. By not giving them attention—and instead focusing on the positive, good feelings I wanted to feel and the happy, confident person I wanted to be—I've begun to taste the freedom that comes with being in my natural state of flow and ease. I now approach problems with curiosity, knowing there's always something to learn and new ways in which to grow.

"By practicing this method and focusing on the positive emotions, all the knowledge I've accumulated that at one point seemed only theoretical is now alive and real. I still find myself reflecting on this and thinking, 'This is too easy. There's no way it's this easy.' And yet, I can't deny the results. I feel different. Opportunities are coming into my life in new, unexpected ways. I'm not saying my life is now magically perfect. I still have problems, but I've changed the way I view them, and I find myself smiling and simply enjoying life rather than being weighed down by worry and stress. I'm excited to continue using BBE and experience the freedom that comes from making real changes in how I perceive myself and the world around me."

—Nate Myers

BBE Is a Process

I will walk you through each of the four steps to use BBE in chapter 4, but I'd like to start here by giving you an overview of what you can expect when going through the process.

First, you will set a goal and a completion date. You'll then list a few benefits you (and others in your life) will receive in reaching your goal, and a few emotions you will be feeling in the days, weeks, or months after reaching that goal and attaining those benefits.

You will then accumulate enough of the emotions you will be feeling after you have achieved your goal (i.e., after your completion date) to outweigh the emotions that are holding your false ideas in place.

Once your false ideas have been outweighed, they will be exposed as false. And when your incredible mind sees they are false, it will quickly eliminate and permanently discard them. With those false ideas gone, it will be very easy for you to achieve your goal.

Your First Step

I will now ask you to spend two to three hours and prepare yourself to use BBE by listening to "The Strangest Secret" a few times. As you will see, the main messages of "The Strangest Secret" are the following:

1. You have far more ability than you can possibly imagine.
2. You become what you think about.
3. Thinking in the same way will hold you back.
4. Conforming—acting like everyone else, without knowing where you're going or why—will make change difficult.
5. To change your results and actions, you need to change your thinking.
6. Goals will help you to think differently.
7. Seeing yourself doing what you will be doing after reaching your goal will help you act differently.

8. This will also help you start moving forward.
9. The easiest way to change your actions is to first change how you think.
10. Seek outside help and motivation.
11. Think good thoughts about yourself.
12. Use the thirty-day test to keep yourself moving forward.
13. You are rewarded in life for rendering service to others.
14. Worry about rendering more service, and the rewards will follow.
15. Rather than competing, it is easier to be more creative.
16. Keep on keeping on.

Remember, you're not required to do this first step before using BBE, but I know that it will give you your best chance at success. I believe in choices. The more choices we have, the better decisions we make. But our false ideas limit our choices. Some tell us we cannot do things we have the ability to do. Others tell us we do not want to do things that are in our best interest to do. The more false ideas we accumulate, the less choices we have. The more we remove those false ideas through BBE, the more choices we have. In addition, and even more importantly, the more *truth* we have. The more truth we have in our lives, the happier we will be.

You can choose to listen to "The Strangest Secret" right now, and keep listening to it as you read this book. Or, you can take a chance and see if using BBE on its own will be enough to allow you to achieve your goal.

We are all different, and many of us have no desire to put in the work to make any changes. Preparing to use BBE is a commitment, and not everyone will be willing to make that effort. Even though it is based on natural laws that always work, and I am promising that using BBE can save you years of time in the future, for some, the reward will not feel like it is worth the time. Keep in mind that there are over seven hundred hours in a month and over eight thousand hours in a year. Spending two to three hours to guarantee your success in saving months or years of time is a good return for that extra time. The biggest risk you face is missing the opportunity to find a tool as effective as BBE at increasing the quality of your life.

It is like taking a test in college. If you take the time to prepare before you take the test, your chance of success will be very high. But, if you fail to attend class and do not study for the test, your chance of success will be very low. If you take the time to listen to the recording, I am confident you will succeed in using BBE. Those two or three hours will save you years in the future. If your desire to succeed is not strong enough to spend that time improving who you are, then BBE is probably not for you.

Testimonial

"I am thrilled to share my profound experience with Bob Raybould's groundbreaking theories on using emotions to transform your life. Believing by Emotions, which involves imagining a better future and allowing oneself to emotionally dwell in that envisioned state, has been incredibly powerful in my own life.

"By employing Bob's method, I have witnessed remarkable changes. The process of identifying and removing the false, limiting thoughts that naturally hinder our ability to dream has been liberating. It has allowed me to see a brighter future with clarity and hope. As I embraced this envisioned future emotionally, I found myself gradually accepting this new reality on a deep, emotional level.

"This emotional acceptance of a brighter future has had a transformative impact on my life. It has enabled me to become the person I always was, buried beneath layers of doubt and limiting beliefs. Bob Raybould's theories have truly empowered me to embrace a new reality and to experience life with renewed purpose and joy.

"I wholeheartedly recommend BBE to anyone seeking profound and lasting change in their lives. Bob's insights and techniques are not only powerful but also life-changing."

—Jared Bauer

In the beginning, almost everyone will face the same hurdle when attempting to use BBE. Many of us have a lot of false ideas that will tell us not to use BBE because it involves using emotions. Over the course of our lives, we have been taught to be logical and to be careful with our emotions, which can cloud our judgment, make us vulnerable, and lead to potentially dangerous mistakes. Instead, we learned to pride ourselves on being dependable, reliable, consistent, and trustworthy. At first, we might fear that using our emotions will interfere with our ability to uphold these qualities. But, in reality, having more truth in our lives will help us with all of these qualities—and BBE is a powerful way to gain more truth.

Emotions are like gasoline, dynamite, electricity, or fire. They can be used to create valuable results, and they can be used to create harmful results. Emotions enable you to use BBE and create value in your life. In the beginning, your emotions will attempt to keep you from using BBE, because they are still tied to your limiting false beliefs. Your emotions will make the process seem scary and dangerous. While this can be a frustrating dilemma, you can view it simply as a terrific demonstration of the power of your emotions. Your emotions are what you will be fighting against as you begin to use BBE. And they are also the factor that makes BBE so powerful and so beneficial.

Emotions are neither good nor bad; they are just emotions. The meaning we place on them is dependent on what we do with them. Love, anger, fear, hate, and all other emotions can either help us move forward or they can hold us back. Take fear, for example. If you were to find yourself in a burning building, fear would compel you to run to safety. This is a true and beneficial use of this emotion. On the other hand, fear may be keeping you from trying BBE because a false idea has convinced you that you are destined to fail. This is a detrimental use of this emotion, and it is holding you back from achieving your goals. In both cases, the emotion in play is fear, but each scenario has a very different result. Truth helps you move forward, and false ideas hold you back. BBE is a way to help your mind expose false ideas and let them go.

Listening to "The Strangest Secret" six to eight times may be enough to help you overcome whatever emotions are holding you back. Rereading this section will also help.

Why Is BBE So Powerful?

There are two reasons for this. The first has to do with our incredible minds. We are all wired in a way that causes us to act in harmony with the way we currently see ourselves. We do not act in harmony with who we are. We do not act in harmony with the DNA we were born with. We do not act in harmony with our talents and abilities. Instead, we act in harmony with our current view of ourselves. That view is formed by our experiences and by accepting the false ideas that have been passed on to us by our parents and others.

When our false ideas are still in place, we view ourselves as someone who will have trouble succeeding, or someone who is going to fail. To keep us acting in harmony with the way we see ourselves, our minds make sure that is what happens. In addition, because we are all connected to one another, our minds work to keep others from helping us.

When we use BBE and see ourselves as someone who has already succeeded—the above factors are reversed. Now, our minds are helping us succeed. In my experience, we also create a new, successful version of ourselves that is gently but firmly pulling us toward our goal. Our minds also reach out and gain the help of others. This makes succeeding much easier and much more pleasant.

The second and biggest reason BBE works is because, once we see ourselves as someone who has already succeeded, our higher power can help us without violating our freedom to choose. Remember, our higher power will not force us to do anything against our will. If our current self-view is different than the one we will have after we've achieved our goal, then if our higher power were to help us, we would be forced to change and become someone different. Our higher power will not do that. But once we have modified our self-view to see ourselves as already having achieved our goal, our higher power can help us get there. With our higher power helping us, the process is much easier. This also strengthens our connection to the world around us, whether that's with our friends and loved ones, our communities, or even the kindness of strangers. Tapping into this rich interconnectedness is only possible when we view ourselves as being worthy of receiving its rewards. If our false ideas have convinced us that we cannot succeed, then we block ourselves from forces that can help us. If we reverse this, then our interconnectedness can come to our aid, and once we have this assistance, we can accomplish any objective we were born with the ability to do.

BBE only allows us to remove our false ideas and modify our self-view in one area of our lives at a time. But, in time, we can adjust our self-view and achieve more of our objectives. Knowing that we can succeed once we have gained this outside assistance makes it much easier for us to keep accumulating emotions throughout the BBE process.

We were each born with different talents and abilities, and as we use BBE, we will each succeed in our own unique way. Because I believe in the following, I feel that BBE can be of value to everyone:

- We all have more abilities and talents than we are using.
- We all have false ideas that are holding us back.
- We all have an inaccurate view of who we are.
- We can all gain more help from our incredible minds.
- We can all gain more help from our higher power.
- We can all gain more help from the world around us.
- We can all experience success more rapidly.

- We can all have more happiness in our journeys forward.

I hope that you will give BBE a chance to improve your life.

TWO

More Success, More Happiness

BELIEVING BY EMOTIONS, BBE, IS a tool that can make your journey through life easier and happier. As I explained in the previous chapter, I discovered BBE after I had failed at selling life insurance, and it enabled me to succeed at an aggressive goal and then continue to succeed beyond my expectations.

Over the years, I've shared this tool with others who have experienced the changes firsthand. (You'll read testimonials from some of them throughout this book.) I taught it to my iPhone salesperson, who was struggling to get an internship. He went on to get five offers and several other incredible accomplishments in just a few months. My grandson was struggling with anxiety, and I shared BBE with him. He still has small bouts of anxiety, but he rapidly succeeded at two jobs and is now successful in business for himself. The tool has assisted all three of us—and many others—to move forward professionally, become better people, and strengthen their faith in their higher power. It will enable you to move forward in all areas of your life, too.

You will accomplish goals and objectives in a fraction of the time it would take you if you were using traditional growth methods. More importantly, BBE will help you love your higher power, yourself, and others more—and your journey toward success will be more enjoyable. And, once you achieve your first goal, you will go on in that area of your life to achieve goals beyond your wildest expectations.

BBE: A New Approach to Growth

BBE is a process of growth that is different from traditional growth in a number of ways.

In traditional growth, we do the work and gain the results we desire. This new success changes the way we see ourselves. I call this approach DO, RESULTS, BE. Here, we confront our false ideas and fight against them, and this process continues during the entire journey, making it a frustrating and painful experience. It can sometimes be so painful that we even give up altogether. And, even when we do achieve our goal, our understanding of our potential is not fully expanded; some of our false ideas have been fought through and overcome, but others are still limiting our view of our full potential. We may even feel like an imposter for a period of time. So, with traditional growth, if we do succeed, we have one successful experience when that happens, but the journey is not a happy one, and feeling like an impostor is not an enjoyable experience.

In comparison, BBE is based on undeniable laws of nature. With BBE, the majority of the work of changing the way we see ourselves and feel about ourselves is completed before we take any physical action working toward our goals. I call this approach BE, DO, RESULTS. How does this work? Our minds act in harmony with the way we see ourselves. By first changing the way we see ourselves (BE), we enable our minds and our higher power to help us act differently (DO) to achieve our goals (RESULTS). This is an incredibly powerful combination that makes an enormous difference. We still do the required work and gain the growth that comes from succeeding, but with BBE, much of that growth happens in the beginning as we remove our false ideas to more accurately see who we really are.

We can liken traditional growth to traveling in an old-fashioned stagecoach, where the journey is bumpy and uncomfortable, and it seems to take forever to reach our destination. On the other hand, using BBE is like traveling in a jet plane, where we're soaring confidently through the sky and will reach our destination in what feels like mere minutes. Which way would you prefer to travel?

Whether we're using traditional growth or BBE, we are exactly the same person with the same DNA, talents, and abilities. But our journey forward—and

BELIEVING BY EMOTIONS

our results—will be very different depending on which method we choose. Most importantly, by choosing to use BBE, we will feel greater happiness throughout our journey.

A good example of traditional growth is given in Dr. Amy Cuddy's TED Talk presentation, "Your Body Language May Shape Who You Are," which you can watch on YouTube. There are many different types of traditional growth. The type Dr. Cuddy used was the "fake it till you make it" approach. In her example, she followed the DO, RESULTS, BE model.

In her presentation, Dr. Cuddy explains how an accident had convinced her that she was far less than she once was. Her self-view was reduced. Before her accident, she had seen herself as a successful person. She had felt confident that she would succeed. In her mind, if the accident had not happened, she would have easily gone on to great success. But, when the accident happened, it changed the way she saw herself. For a time, she saw herself as someone who would not succeed.

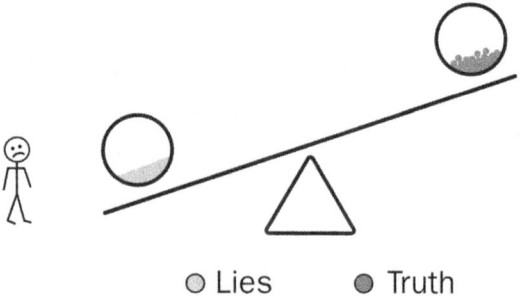

Then, she was able to use the "fake it till you make it" approach to overcome and push aside the false ideas that had been created by her accident, and she went on to have great success.

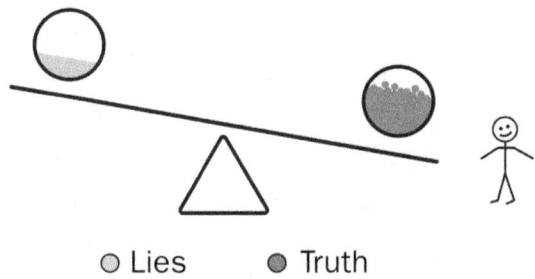

○ Lies   ● Truth

But, even after achieving significant success, she still felt like an imposter. During that period of time, deep down, a part of her still felt like the person who was not able to achieve success. It took her a couple more years to see herself as a success.

I have my own story of following a traditional path to growth. I did not experience an accident, like in Dr. Cuddy's story. Rather, I have dyslexia, and it caused me to spend two years in the second grade. In addition to my dyslexia (as I will outline in more detail later in the book), my situation at the time of my birth resulted in several experiences that severely lowered my self-view. This all caused me to believe that I was dumb. For many years, I saw myself as a dumb person.

But I was able to use traditional growth methods to fight through my false ideas and change my behaviors, even while I still thought of myself as being dumb. After a long time of doing this, I finally improved in my schoolwork, and I no longer believed that I was dumb. However, this process took many years, and I did not feel that I was really smart until I started working for a large corporation in New York. They only hired engineers from the top one-third of their classes. When I took a test they gave to those engineers, my score on the test put me in the top 5 percent of engineers who had graduated in the top one-third of their classes. And this helped me go from feeling that I was dumb to learning that I was smart and good at solving complex problems.

And, while I did ultimately achieve my goal, the process could have been much faster and more enjoyable if I had used the BBE system back then.

What Makes BBE Different?

Believing by Emotions is very different from traditional growth. In BBE, the first step is to change the way we see ourselves. Instead of DO, RESULTS, BE, the order in BBE is BE, DO, RESULTS. We first use BBE to see ourselves as the person we will be after we have achieved our goal. This enables us to more happily take action toward achieving our goals. Achieving our goals is then simply an expression of who we are.

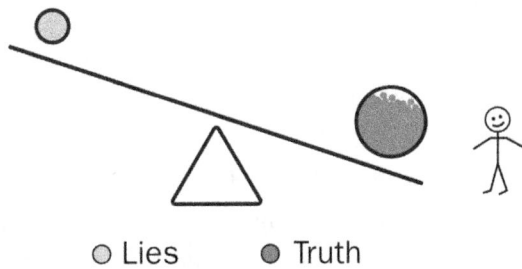

I discovered this in 1968. Prior to that, in 1964, I had received my MBA from the University of Utah. Rather than take a job with a large corporation, I decided to be my own boss and sell life insurance. After fifteen months of working sixty-five hours a week and not making much progress, I quit. I decided I was not cut out to be a life insurance salesman. Instead, I used my MBA to obtain a job with the corporation in New York. It was there where I took the engineering test that convinced me I really was smart.

During my two and a half years with that corporation, I read everything I could to help me succeed in selling. I wanted to be a successful life insurance salesman and be my own boss. I had already failed once at this, and I was trying to get enough information to enable me to succeed on my second try. When I had finally built up enough confidence to return to selling life insurance, I left New York and moved back to Salt Lake City in 1968.

As I mentioned in chapter 1, it was at this time when I began listening to Earl Nightingale's "The Strangest

BELIEVING BY EMOTIONS

Secret" every time I was alone in my car. Following the directions given in the recording, I set a goal to significantly increase the annual income I had been earning in New York, and to do so within thirty months.

The recording was perfect. It did not ask me to see myself as a successful insurance salesperson. I had already tried and failed at doing that. I had no idea what my being a successful insurance salesman would look like.

Instead, the recording prompted me to picture myself doing what I would do *after* I had reached my goal. Doing this would help me think differently about myself.

My goal was to quadruple my income. Driving a Porsche was what I would be doing after I had reached my goal. So I went to the nearest car dealership and sat in the driver's seat of a Porsche 911 coupe. As I sat down and wrapped my hands around the steering wheel, I discovered BBE.

A surge of excitement, gratitude, and happiness coursed through me. I was feeling how I would feel while driving my own Porsche 911 after I've reached my goal. I began to *feel* like a person who drives a Porsche.

These emotions took me by surprise, and I savored them for a good, long while. A salesman came over and asked me if I would like to go for a test-drive. I said no. I just wanted to sit there and feel those wonderful feelings.

Those feelings opened the door in my mind and allowed me to see myself differently. I was filled with a new level of truth about myself. I didn't know it at the time, but I was experiencing new laws of nature in my own life. I was beginning to feel like a successful person. I was now ready to change the order and create a method of self-improvement that would be totally different from traditional growth; I was ready to see myself as a success *before* I started working toward my goal. BE, DO, RESULTS would be my path forward.

Listening to "The Strangest Secret" opened my heart and mind. It taught me that, if I can change my thoughts, I can change my actions. That gave me hope. But it did not change the way I felt about myself. My false ideas had still controlled me at that time. When I had previously set my goal, I'd changed the way I was *thinking*. But, when I sat in the Porsche, I was changing the way I was *feeling*. This change enabled me to accumulate enough positive emotions to outweigh the negative emotions that had been holding my false ideas in place. This had been impossible for me to do when I was using traditional methods of growth and relying on intellectual arguments.

Before I sat down in the Porsche, my self-view as an unsuccessful person had been firmly in place. I had the ability to succeed, but my emotions were holding my self-view in place and telling me I could not succeed. That was a lie. If I continued to believe that lie, success would have remained beyond my grasp. My faulty self-view, not my truth, would have remained totally in control.

But, by sitting in the Porsche, I had expanded that idea. I began to accumulate the feelings I would be experiencing *after* I had reached my goal. Sitting in that

BELIEVING BY EMOTIONS

car and feeling those feelings for ten or fifteen minutes was enough to cause me to gain enough truth to believe that I could succeed. I was feeling the emotions I'd feel in the months after achieving my goal; I was feeling like a successful person, like someone who drove a Porsche. Absolutely nothing in my life had changed; I was still struggling to succeed. But I was beginning to feel how I would feel after I had succeeded. I was not yet convinced that I would succeed, but I believed that I was capable of succeeding. I had made the initial flip of the scale in my mind.

Now, over fifty-five years later, I understand what was happening to me at that time. I was beginning to discover and understand these new natural laws. Those new feelings started to change the way I saw myself. They began to expose my false ideas as imposters. I had the ability to succeed; I had always had the ability to succeed. But my false ideas had been keeping me from seeing these truths. The more of these emotions I accumulated, the more I exposed my false ideas. My mind then eliminated those false ideas—and I saw my true self. I had already accomplished enough in my life that I did not see myself as a loser. But my false ideas had been keeping me from seeing how much of a winner I am. And if that was not enough, my higher power began to give me assistance both directly and indirectly. With the assistance I was receiving from my mind and my higher power, I knew I could not fail. And if I did fail, it would simply mean that my higher power had something even better in store for me. I just needed to trust that the natural laws behind BBE were there to help me. Doing this enabled me to enjoy my journey forward.

"The Strangest Secret" and other methods of traditional growth also probably work based on natural laws. If you spend enough time seeing yourself doing what you will be doing after you have reached your goal, your motivation will eventually reach the point at which you can effectively fight through the false ideas that are holding you back. That is how different types of traditional growth work; our false ideas have power over us, and we need to gain additional personal power to fight through them.

BBE uses a different natural law. It does not make you any more powerful or give you more strength, determination, or persistence to fight through your false ideas. Instead, it is based on the law that if you accumulate enough emotions to outweigh and expose your false ideas, you will modify your self-view in regard to your goal *before* you do any work. You will know you can succeed before you begin, rather than gaining this knowledge at some point after you've succeeded. And you will not need any additional personal power to fight through your blocks, because they will already have been removed.

Until you understand this difference, you will keep trying to make BBE the same as the other growth methods you have used in the past. But it is different. I get it; we have all moved forward at one point in our lives by using traditional growth. It works sometimes, and we are all glad it does. These methods have helped you achieve some goals in the past. But why wouldn't you choose the path that is easier, faster, and more enjoyable?

Almost all of us have had experiences that have reduced our self-esteem and introduced limiting beliefs into our lives. We have all also inherited false ideas from our ancestors. Almost all of us have accepted false ideas from others, and we've added those to our accumulation of false ideas that have reduced our self-view. We are all winners, and the more truth we gain, the more we will see that fact.

These false ideas only exist as long as we believe them. Once we expose them as false, we will cease to believe them. Once we stop believing them, they will fade away and lose their power over us.

Another View

An easy way to help you understand the difference between traditional growth and BBE is to look at an example from the digital world where traditional growth would be likened to linear computing and BBE would be likened to quantum computing.

For example, if we have a briefcase that has a nine-digit combination lock, there is an almost infinite number of possible solutions we'll have to try before we find the one combination that will open the briefcase. The time it will take to reach the correct answer will be very different depending on whether we use linear computing or quantum computing.

When using linear computing, the computer will try each potential solution one by one. It could almost take as long as the universe has been around to solve the problem.

But, when using quantum computing, the computer will create a thousand imaginary briefcases that will work in tandem, with each one tackling a fraction of the problem. This would take about six and a half minutes.

Traditional growth is a step-by-step method of moving forward, much like linear computing. We are on our own, going one step at a time, fighting against our false ideas and our minds as they work to keep us from achieving our goals. The process is slow and difficult.

BBE is a team effort, making it more like quantum computing. With BBE, we quickly change our self-view, eliminate our false ideas, and replace them with truth before we begin our journey. This enables our incredible minds and our higher power to help us succeed. (Our higher power has more capability and knowledge than a whole group of quantum computers.) With this winning team, we can advance toward our goal on multiple levels simultaneously, and we can achieve success exponentially faster than if we were using traditional growth—plus, we're happier along the way.

Leveling the Playing Field

Another key difference between BBE and traditional methods of growth is that BBE makes success available to *everyone*. You might find yourself doubting whether this tool will work for you. Maybe you've come to believe that only someone with a successful background, high self-esteem, a large amount of self-discipline and self-determination, or great willpower and persistence can create a successful life.

Well, when it comes to using traditional methods of growth, there might be a select few who are strong enough to succeed by fighting through their false ideas.

But BBE changes everything. Everyone can modify their self-view. Most of us will need to start with a small goal, but we can all do it. With BBE, once we adjust our self-view, *everyone* can experience a faster, more enjoyable path to success. Everyone can have more happiness in their journey. It takes a much lower level of self-discipline, persistence, determination, and willpower to use BBE and accumulate enough emotions to eliminate your false ideas and gain more truth.

With BBE, everyone can be successful, believe more deeply, and feel happier in a short period of time. The playing field is much more level than it ever has been. We can all gain more truth in our lives easily and rapidly.

Testimonial

"When Bob Raybould first told me about Believing by Emotions, I was intrigued. I had tried countless self-improvement techniques in the past and had experienced some growth, but it always felt like a long and arduous journey.

"BBE is completely different because the process of accumulating emotions is pleasant and exciting.

> As I envision having already achieved my goal, I feel myself being uplifted and empowered by the positive emotions I've attached to that accomplishment. This sets me up to engage more fully with each day's tasks, and it energizes me to give more of myself in learning, growing, and connecting with others.
>
> "I've also come to some significant realizations about myself while releasing my false ideas. For example, using BBE helped me recognize that I had been holding on to the notion that having a successful business meant that I would have to sacrifice my family life and personal well-being. It turns out that I had picked up this false idea from a few business coaches I had followed, as well as from some of my fellow entrepreneurs, who glamorized the 'never-ending hustle' of running a business. I was able to release this false idea by replacing it with positive emotions such as feeling peaceful, joyful, and grateful. This has shifted how I approach my work, and how I connect with my clients and customers.
>
> "I am so thankful to Bob for sharing BBE with me. It is such a valuable tool, and it has helped me create a more gratifying and abundant life."
>
> —Anna Krusinski

Emotions Are Stronger than Logic

My fifty-plus years of success as a salesman has taught me that most sales, and most important decisions, are made at the emotional level and are then justified with logic. In my personal experience, trying to overcome emotions with logic is like trying to put out a fire with

BELIEVING BY EMOTIONS

a squirt gun. On the other hand, working to overcome even long-held negative emotions with strong positive emotions gives us a great chance of success.

Our past experiences have created beliefs and conclusions that have been stored inside us for a long time and have combined to form the self-view of someone who cannot succeed. This false view has been held in place by our negative emotions.

If we want to change this conclusion—and our current self-view—we need to use our emotions.

When I first came across BBE, sitting in that Porsche created enough good strong emotions to flip the scale and begin to free me from my negative emotions and false ideas. From then on, every time I touched the steering wheel of my Volkswagen Beetle, I felt like I was touching the wheel of that Porsche. Each time I did this, I added more units of emotion to the side of truth.

At that time, I did not understand anything about BBE. I was simply recreating the experience that had taken place when I had sat in the Porsche. I did not realize it at the time, but I was accumulating emotions. All I knew was that doing this felt great. I did not see that I was on my way to success. I had no idea that I had discovered new laws of nature. On some days, I was still filled with doubts. In addition, I could not figure out how I was going to succeed. But I remained consistent and kept accumulating more units of emotion.

Three weeks after I first sat in the Porsche, the biggest change took place. I had been fighting against my doubts all day, and I had gone home feeling discouraged. During the night, the emotions I had been accumulating flipped the scale in an enormous way. As I slept, my mind absolutely concluded that I would succeed. When I woke up, I saw myself as someone who would succeed.

I had no clue how I would succeed, but I *knew* that I would. My new self-view was firmly in place. I was a big-time winner, and I finally knew it. It had taken me three weeks to accumulate enough emotions to totally convince myself that I would succeed.

Now that I knew I would succeed, nothing else mattered. I knew that I was a success, and I knew I would achieve my goal. I would happily do whatever it took; I would work as hard as I needed to work. Once I felt this way, my mind had no choice but to help me, and I also started to receive help from others around me. And when I needed even more help, my higher power guided me in finding the answers I needed to succeed. It was only a matter of time until I succeeded.

I had not changed as a person. I did not have any new DNA. I was the very same person I had been four years earlier when I had gotten so discouraged that I had given up and taken an easier job.

What was the difference? It was this: I had quit believing the lies I had been telling myself. I was the same person, but I had replaced many of my false ideas with truth. I was seeing myself more accurately; I was seeing more of the person my higher power had created me to be. And with my self-view adjusted, my higher power could assist me without violating my freedom of choice.

The fact that I knew I would succeed helped me learn the new skills I needed to succeed. It also helped refine my abilities and my talents. I was still working about sixty-five hours a week, but I was having fun. All day long, I was full of confidence and happiness. And I did ultimately reach my goal.

BBE does not remove our need to do the work. It is simply easier to do the work when our actions become an extension of the way we see ourselves. Attempting to use logic to force ourselves to be someone different is very hard work. (So hard, in fact, that when I first tried to do it, I failed.) Many of you have struggled when fighting against your current self-view in this way. A few of you may have even failed, like I did. But when we harness the power of our emotions by using BBE to modify the way we see ourselves, the journey is easier, faster, and much happier.

Testimonial

"I love self-help books! No matter the topic, I am nearly always the target audience. When it comes to prosperity and success, I have come a long way from being in psychiatric hospitals in my teens and experiencing chronic depression and anxiety in my twenties and thirties. But, despite years of various types of therapy and multiple twelve-step programs, I still felt listless and 'held back' in life. I desperately searched for some other self-help program that could magically fix the rut I was in. However, I didn't realize that what was holding me back was my own false belief system.

"Believing by Emotions has opened me up to a whole world of possibilities. Being asked to think about and meditate on how I will feel after I achieve my goal has put a whole new—but very logical—spin on things for me. Listening to 'The Strangest Secret' a handful of times also helped put BBE in perspective.

"The goal I chose to try was financial stability. Well, in the few short months I have been practicing feeling my future-success feelings, I have more than doubled my income. I also had a blissful aha moment when I realized that life isn't about taking on more work, meeting impossible deadlines, and accomplishing unrealistic goals, but about surrendering to what life is really like at any moment in time.

"Simultaneously with doing BBE—and it cannot be a coincidence—I had a major breakthrough in my faith. I had been raised Jewish but had disowned that and was suspicious of any organized religion. In my twelve-step program, I had accepted that I had some kind of higher power but did not see it as a religious figure. Then, one day, I was offered the opportunity to do two-way prayer for the first time. And what I heard from my higher power was, 'My child …' I discovered that I do have a religious god who loves me as His child. Wow! What a revelation. What a breakthrough. Again, I must say, this cannot be a coincidence that I was also practicing BBE daily at the same time.

"While Bob recommended I spend forty minutes to an hour each day in meditative contemplation, I instead meditated on my positive feelings for several minutes frequently throughout my day, releasing my false emotions in the process. Somehow, BBE was helping me to have hope that financial prosperity would come. It was helping me to think differently about money and success in a way that no twelve-step program or decades of therapy had ever done for me.

"While these positive shifts were beginning to happen, I had a brief period of doubt about BBE. Then I realized that I had skipped a crucial step: I needed something tangible to represent my goal. What I didn't realize until later was that this was my scale-tipping point. This was when I was so sure of my success that I knew I would reach my goal, no matter what. Right then, I used some of my surplus funds (something I'd never had before BBE), and purchased tickets for a trip to California, my home state. Having that tangible ticket in hand was the breakthrough I needed for BBE to take hold.

"I was at the stage of being willing to do whatever it took. I had a few setbacks, but instead of sinking into total panic and fear, I was already feeling the emotions and confidence of financial success. Sure enough, an offer came along for a high-paying job that was much more fun and exciting and would require far less time and effort, which meant I would be able to stay solvent without having to work so many hours.

> "BBE has changed my thinking … and my life. I am obsessed with this process! I can't wait to use BBE on a new goal! It works. It really does!"
>
> —Leya Booth

Overcoming the Doubt

As I have been using BBE over the last fifty-five years, this sequence has been consistent. Just before I accumulate enough emotions to know that I will succeed, my false ideas put up a last-ditch effort to stay in control. It is like they are real voices that do not want to be silenced. I am filled with doubts and discouragement, and I am tempted to give up.

In these situations, I just trust that BBE will work, because I know that natural laws always work. I keep accumulating emotions. Not long after I show my commitment to continue accumulating emotions, BBE works, and I am even more confident of my future success. (The first few times this happened, I was bothered by it, and continuing to accumulate emotions was difficult, but I did it anyway. But it has happened so often that now I just smile to myself because I know that I will soon be filled with happiness. Soon after that, I always feel I am ready to do whatever it takes to succeed.)

This will be especially true for you the first time you use BBE. You will be fighting against two groups of false ideas: those that are preventing you from using BBE, and those that are keeping you from achieving your goal. They are both fighting to continue to exist. Once you stop believing in them, they will no longer exist. Believe me, it is worth the extra effort. No one likes to be controlled, especially by false ideas.

As you continue to use BBE, the doubts will come up again and again. They are trying to say in place. These strong feelings that are holding you back do not want to be eliminated. The bigger the step forward you will ultimately take, the more emotions you will need to accumulate. But the changes in your self-view and confidence when you finally accumulate enough positive emotions will be worth whatever commitment and time it takes.

In traditional growth methods, our false ideas fight to stay alive during the whole journey. In my experience, when using a traditional approach, many of my false ideas stayed alive even after I had experienced success and moved forward. Instead of removing them, I had just found a way around them.

With BBE, we remove the great majority of our false ideas before we begin the journey. For this reason, our false ideas may not recognize that they are at risk of being eliminated until those final few days or hours. This has repeatedly been my experience.

THREE

The Power of the Future with BBE

ONE OF THE INCREDIBLE ADVANTAGES of using Believing by Emotions is that our growth can continue endlessly after we achieve our first goal. Once our lies and false ideas are removed, they stay removed—and our future goals become easier to achieve.

About two years after I first sat in that Porsche, I was driving my very own Porsche, and I was living in a new home. After another two months, I had quadrupled my earnings. To my great surprise, my understanding of my true potential almost exploded. I could finally see that I had far more potential than I had ever imagined. I knew I could move forward and continue to have additional successes. I did not set another goal, but I continued to accumulate emotions. My income continued to double each year for the next four years. Then, just twelve years after I had discovered BBE, I was financially independent.

BELIEVING BY EMOTIONS

Our growth becomes limitless with BBE because, in addition to removing our false ideas, we are also seeing ourselves in a more positive, empowered light. And, because we are programmed to act in harmony with the way we see ourselves, we act differently and create the results we desire.

The Long-Lasting Power of BBE

BBE has been an important part of my life for over fifty-five years. It has enabled me to accomplish so many goals I could not have accomplished previously. The time I have saved using BBE has created time for me to do things I would have never otherwise had time to do. BBE has saved me *years*. But I will say again that the biggest benefit of using BBE over other popular methods of growth and improvement is the happiness you will enjoy during the journey and after you have succeeded.

As you use BBE, you will find that it will become easier to achieve your goal each time. Because of this, I suggest that you start (in chapter 4) with a small goal and work your way up to bigger goals.

When I first discovered BBE, I was able to increase my income fourfold. If I had gone for a higher, more aggressive goal, I am not confident that I would have been able to overcome the false ideas that were holding me back. In fact, my initial goal was to increase my income sixfold. A good friend told me at the time to reduce it to fourfold. I missed that goal by about two hundred dollars, but I have chosen to call that close enough.

THE POWER OF THE FUTURE WITH BBE

After that, my circumstances continued to improve as I kept using BBE. I was presented with several new opportunities and was able to evolve from being just a great salesman to also becoming an excellent businessman.

In addition to gaining assistance from my own mind by using BBE, what was happening in our country at that time was almost perfectly suited to help me gain great success. In setting my goal to quadruple my income, my higher power knew what was just around the corner. I give my higher power credit for my constantly being in the right place and doing the right thing. This has allowed me to take advantage of the unique opportunities that came my way. I gained a significant advantage by becoming one of the first financial planners in the Intermountain West, and I helped form one of the first tax-sheltered real estate firms in the United States. But, without BBE, I would not have been so confident and would not have progressed so rapidly.

This happened about five years before everyone else figured out the current tax laws for investing in commercial real estate. Five years later, when everyone figured this out, everyone (including the big firms on Wall Street) started raising money to invest in real estate. Firms across the country were buying real estate, and my company was approached by several of them. As we studied these offers and spent time in meditation, we gained the courage to sell all of our real estate investments. This took us about four years to accomplish. Then, two years later, the new tax laws reduced the value of real estate by

BELIEVING BY EMOTIONS

about 25 percent. This series of unexpected events greatly assisted in my incredible success. But BBE allowed me to continue with success after success in the following years.

During the time when we were acquiring real estate, my income continued to double each year over the next four years. This meant that my income doubled six times in six and a half years.

These numbers demonstrate the point I am attempting to make. The initial flipping of the scale takes dedication. But the benefits that follow that dedication far exceed anything we can even think about at the time while we are working to flip the scale toward truth.

The initial increase in my earnings was a 400 percent increase. But, because of the false ideas I had removed, the happiness I was feeling, and the truth I had gained about what I was capable of, my income continued to double again and again. The first increase—although it was the hardest to achieve—was a small fraction of the total increase. But even with all my success, the greatest benefit I received was the increased happiness I experienced both during each journey and thereafter.

Without experiencing this for yourself, it is hard to understand how your view of your potential will explode. Your self-view will expand, and this will enable you to achieve the significant improvements you will be making after you've achieved your first goal.

Keep in mind that each person's level of success will be different. It is rare to be a great salesman. It is also rare to be a great businessman. But it is even more unusual to be both a great salesman *and* a great businessman. I am very lucky to have achieved both traits. I could never have done this on my own. The help I've received from my higher power, and my change in my self-view, caused me to also receive help from many different sources. This is an important fact to remember. The average person reading this will not have the same level of business success that I have had. Not everyone will become rich, but we all have different areas in which we desire to excel, and BBE can help us achieve those goals.

BBE does not give us the power to change other people; everyone is free to choose for themselves. It also does not give us power over circumstances that are beyond our control. But it does enable us to remove our false ideas and become better people by gaining more truth in our lives. The additional help we receive from our higher power will then make success easier, and our increased happiness will enable us to more fully enjoy who we are and our circumstances in life. Everyone using BBE can eliminate enough false ideas to be successful enough to live comfortably. Once we have enough to live comfortably, working to become better people becomes a more purposeful use of our time than just trying to accumulate more and more wealth. Your success will look different from mine, but you will still experience the joy in the process, you will gain more assistance from your higher power, you'll know more of your true self, and you'll find success more easily each time you use BBE.

BELIEVING BY EMOTIONS

My wife once read a book written by Gary Emery, PhD, a psychiatrist who has worked with the top movie stars. In the book, he commented that we all have strengths and weaknesses. He found that the movie stars who were at the top of their profession also had many weaknesses. He concluded that, if we could see everyone's strengths and weaknesses, we would see that we all are about average people. I would agree. Almost everything mechanical or electrical I have tried to fix has ended up worse than when I began. I not only can't fix it, but I make it worse. For example, I worked for several days installing a new part on a car but ended up with three or four leftover parts that I did not know what to do with. Even though we are all about average, I still believe that everyone who uses BBE will not only succeed and find greater happiness, but that their initial success will open the door to other successes beyond their current expectations.

That is a very bold claim. The following testimonial supports that claim.

> **Testimonial**
>
> "Believing by Emotions has been a transformative force in my life, not only guiding me through incredible personal and professional milestones but also deepening my connection with God. Before discovering BBE, I was like many others—caught in a cycle of limited successes and frustrating setbacks. I knew I had potential, but I couldn't quite harness it. More

importantly, I felt distant from the true source of all power and wisdom: God Himself.

"Everything changed when I embraced the principles of BBE. By eliminating the false ideas and emotional barriers that had been holding me back, I not only gained clarity and confidence in my abilities, but I also drew closer to God in a way I had never experienced before. This shift in mindset allowed me to trust Him fully, unlocking His power and favor in my life. I began to see that success wasn't just about my own efforts; it was about aligning my emotions and beliefs with His truth.

"As a result, I experienced an unprecedented increase in my income, effectively doubling each year for a number of successive years. But more than financial success, I experienced spiritual renewal. This newfound faith and freedom gave me the courage to pursue my long-held dream of starting an investment company. The principles of BBE didn't just help me build wealth; they taught me how to walk in God's purpose, relying on His strength rather than my own.

"Today, I'm blessed to manage over 100 million dollars' worth of real estate—a testament not only to the power of BBE but to the power of faith in God. By removing limiting beliefs and aligning my heart with His promises, I have seen His grace, wisdom, and guidance at every step. My success is not just financial; it's a reflection of a life transformed by faith. I am happier, more confident, and more at peace than I ever imagined, knowing that God is at the center of it all.

BELIEVING BY EMOTIONS

> "For anyone feeling stuck, overwhelmed, or simply wanting to elevate their life, I wholeheartedly recommend BBE. More importantly, I encourage you to seek God in the process. When you align your beliefs and emotions with His truth, you'll unlock a level of success, joy, and purpose that goes beyond your wildest dreams."
>
> —Sam Froerer

In experiencing the long-term benefits of using BBE, you will also find that your journey becomes smoother. Life can be likened to riding a bicycle. If we keep moving forward, it is easier for us to keep our balance. The slower we go, the harder it is to keep our balance. This is a good description of what happens when you use BBE. Throughout your life, you had accumulated so many false ideas that the hill you were riding up was very steep. You may have even lost your balance and given up on your goals. But, by using BBE, you first accumulate enough emotions to remove your false ideas. And, with the false ideas removed, the hill becomes very gentle. It may still have a few steep parts, but your momentum and the help you are receiving from your higher power will be strong enough when you reach these that going over them will be pleasant and you will be able to maintain your balance. Achieving your goals will become fun and easy. And, best of all, you will feel happier during and after the journey.

FOUR

Using BBE

WHEN I FIRST BEGAN DRAFTING this book, I was hoping just to write a booklet. I wanted to provide others with a quick fix for finding happiness and improved results. I had no idea I had discovered natural laws, absolute truths, that would make change and growth easier. But, as I gained a deeper understanding of the power of Believing by Emotions, I knew that I needed to expand this book to give everyone enough information to understand BBE well enough that they could begin using the tool right away. In this chapter, I'll cover the ins and outs of the four steps of this process.

Remember, the benefits come after challenging work. In traditional growth, the hard work happens during the journey. But, with BBE, the hard work happens mostly in the beginning as you accumulate emotions and eliminate the majority of your false ideas. That hard work will bring you benefits—including increased happiness—far beyond your expectations.

Choosing Your Goal

I am now going to ask you to choose a goal for your first time using BBE. The goal you choose is not nearly as important as the fact that you are beginning to use BBE. But the more emotional drive behind your goal, the easier it will be to accumulate your emotions.

In chapter 1, I asked you to prepare yourself to use BBE by listening to Earl Nightingale's "The Strangest Secret" multiple times. In this chapter, you will now be given the opportunity to use BBE to eliminate the false ideas that are holding you back.

To succeed, you will first need to set a reasonable goal. It should focus on one area of your life where you want to feel more happiness, and it should be something you know you can accomplish within a few days or weeks. Assuming you choose a goal you have the ability to achieve, once you use BBE to modify your self-view and remove your false ideas, your journey will be happy, easy, and rapid—and your success will be assured.

When I first discovered BBE, I was desperate to succeed, and I chose a very large goal. In hindsight, I also recognize that, at that time, part of me thought that what Earl Nightingale was suggesting in "The Strangest Secret" was too good to be true. And, back then, I loved being right, to the point that I was willing to fail just so I could prove that what the recording was saying was too good to be true. You may have some of the same feelings about what I am writing here. Thankfully, a good friend helped me change my goal and settle on one I could achieve.

You may also be tempted to pick a goal that is all about tangible results (for example, increasing your income or finding a new job). But it's important that your goal also has an emotional drive behind it that you can focus on. For example, when I first discovered BBE, I had no idea that the main benefit I would be gaining was more happiness in my life. Instead, my focus was on being successful and earning more money. I mistakenly thought more income would make me happier. Over time, the more I used BBE, the more I was able to appreciate that the true value was in enjoying the journey toward increased income. It took me years to come to this realization, and I'm sharing it with you now to save you that time. Select your first goal based on a tangible result that will also drive you emotionally through the process.

In 2004, when I was working with the University of Utah football team to help them use BBE, I had improved my understanding of BBE and started small in working with just a few players. I had success with this small group. The coach, Urban Meyer, then asked me to work with six of his players in the offseason. I worked with them in depth using BBE and had them listen to "The Strangest Secret." I then helped those players feel how they would be feeling after they'd improved their individual skills. The team went on to a high final ranking and an undefeated season, and four of the six players I worked with went on to play in the NFL (one decided football was not for him, and the other remained a significant contributor to the team). The credit goes foremost to the team and the coaches, but I do feel I was a small part of their success.

In setting your own goal, remember that the bigger the goal, the more feelings you will need to accumulate. Because of this, I suggest you choose a goal that is important but can be attained in a few days or weeks. Spend some time thinking about it, but not too much time. It does not need to be a perfect goal. Whatever reasonable goal you choose, you will find happiness in your journey and you will have a tool that will give you happiness in your future journey. BBE gives you a tool to achieve one reasonable goal after another. Once you have achieved your first goal, the door will be open for much additional success. The key is to choose a goal that will help you succeed.

Below are a few testimonials from people who have used BBE on small goals. The first was written by someone who has successfully used BBE on a goal that had eluded him for a long time. The second one comes from someone who has been working on his goals for years but only started writing them down when he tried using BBE—and he finally started seeing results. The last testimonial is by someone who has been working on his goals with BBE for over a year and has kept moving forward.

Testimonial

My friend, Erik Groszyk, played college basketball in the Ivy League and has been using BBE on small, short-term goals.

"Early in our friendship, Bob Raybould had described Believing by Emotions. I've always enjoyed discussing BBE with him because certain aspects of it correspond to certain 'discoveries' I've made in my own life over the years. Since I was a teenager, I have practiced positive thinking and visualization. While these techniques have helped me find success and happiness in life, my conversations with Bob clarified areas where my beliefs about myself and my goals could be further refined.

"Bob extended a small suggestion to me: that I pick a small goal to begin experimenting with his theory of BBE. The goal that has deepened my understanding of BBE the most was the desire to make ten consecutive free throws on the basketball court. This is something I did so regularly as a young person, I hardly thought much of it at the time. However, as I now play basketball less often, it is something I rarely accomplish anymore. A free throw is a very simple shot—you are stationary (as opposed to moving quickly), you are lined up perfectly straight just fifteen feet from the basket, and there is no defender to rush you or alter your shot. However, all these factors can actually lead even the most experienced professional to overthink their shot. Historically, even the greatest shooters will make this shot about 90 percent of the time, while even good shooters by professional standards might make this shot just 70 to 80 percent of the time in games. The poorest shooters will make it less than 50 percent of the time (worse than a coin toss).

"I could not remember the last time I had made ten free throws in a row, even though I'd tried most of the times that I went to the gym. It was not because of lack of ability, but there was some mental block preventing me from achieving the delicate balance of focus and relaxation sometimes called 'flow state.' I thought this would be perfect for testing Bob's theory of BBE.

"Within a couple days of doing BBE, I could simply access the emotions in my mind and allow them to permeate my body. Previously, during my shooting practices, I would visualize the ball going through the net; this was a habit I had developed as a teenager. Only through working with BBE did I realize that this technique had been incomplete. I could imagine the outcome of a successful free throw attempt—the ball cleanly falling through the net—but still have the emotional experience (anxiety) of missing a shot. In this way, the image I was visualizing was in conflict with the emotions I hoped to achieve, and BBE clarified this discordance for me. In fact, I realized that visualizing the ball going through the rim was actually less important than experiencing the satisfaction and joy that this outcome would provide to me.

"Bob had told me many times that the key to BBE was to actually experience the emotions of achieving your goal in a visceral way, but I had not thought to replace other aspects of my visualization with simply experiencing emotions. As far as identifying the benefits of accomplishing my goal, I believe this had a clarifying effect in my mind. It forced me to think more about *why* I desired a certain outcome, which served to further convince me of its personal importance, and it also helped me contextualize my goal as an intermediate step in my larger journey as an athlete. This helped reconcile a dichotomy that relates to our goals: we are trying to accomplish something that challenges us now, but will seem very simple to the future version of ourselves. (And, in this particular case, it was previously easy to a *past* version of myself.)

"A week after beginning BBE, I successfully made ten free throws in a row with seemingly little difficulty. I could not remember how many years it had been since I'd done this, and it felt like an enormous triumph—not over some vaunted opponent, but over my own biased, counterproductive thinking. When I did it again a few days later, it felt so casual that I hardly thought about it. By this point, my mind no longer treated it as some insurmountable task, but as an inevitable outcome. The anxiety and mental chatter I had previously experienced—especially after making seven, eight, or nine shots in a row—had mostly dissipated. Success, as they say, became a habit for me in this small regard. This entire experience has helped further clarify the power of the mind, and it's led me to wonder ... what other tricks is my mind playing on me?"

—Erik Groszyk

Testimonial

I have shared BBE with John Lund, and he has received value from simply writing down his goals on his BBE sheet.

"I have had the pleasure of knowing Bob Raybould for more than twenty years. Bob has been an important mentor in my life, both personally and in business. I feel fortunate that Bob has shared Believing by Emotions with me. I have benefited tremendously from these principles.

"When Bob first asked me to follow very specific directions to put BBE to the test, he asked me to write down a single goal that I was confident that I have the natural ability to accomplish and could achieve within a few weeks.

"My first thought regarding this task was simple; I certainly don't need to write this goal down on paper! This is a goal that I think about every minute of every day of my life! Why write it on paper? I was happy, however, to do this for Bob, as he is a dear friend and mentor.

"I pulled out a sheet of paper and began to write my goal. I was amazed at the emotion I felt as I did this! Writing my goal with ink and paper took my goal to a whole new level emotionally. *Wow!* I had never felt these emotions like I did when I committed them to writing! I felt these emotions as if my goal were already accomplished!

"Although this entire experience lasted only a few minutes, it was profound and touched me to my core. The difference? Committing this simple goal to writing made it absolutely real to me.

"As I was using this tool regularly, I began to view myself differently. I quickly realized that I was beginning to see myself as God sees me. With each experience and success, my personal view of myself became closer to the way God sees me. With this new perspective, it became nearly impossible to fail.

"I *never* would have guessed that using pen and paper would make such a profound difference. I will forever use this powerful tool in my life. Thank you, Bob!"

—John Lund

Testimonial

Andy Robertson is a business associate whom I have known for several years. As he recounts below, he has been enjoying the long-term, cumulative benefits of using BBE regularly.

"I'm truly overwhelmed with my results from Believing by Emotions, especially given how little time and effort it requires.

"After much hemming and hawing, I finally drafted a list of goals that had already been bouncing around my head for some time. They were not new, as I had been thinking about them for many years. I then made time to quietly review my list every morning before my day got busy.

BELIEVING BY EMOTIONS

> "Within a few short days, I'm here to tell you that I had surprisingly strong feelings of confidence, determination, and happiness. From a logical perspective, it makes sense to me that the concept of repeatedly focusing on something will keep it top of mind. However, I wasn't prepared for the clarity of positive emotions inside my head and heart. It was empowering. And I was in awe.
>
> "In the beginning, these feelings weren't there if I didn't look at my list. Now that it's been a year of using BBE, I can unlock the same empowering feelings when I mentally slow down for a few moments and focus on how I'll feel when achieving my goals. These feelings fade without intentional action on my part, so my challenge is to regularly make time to do the work. All of this has reinforced that BBE works for me—and I sincerely hope that it will work for you."
>
> —Andy Robertson

Four Steps to Success

Although using BBE requires time and commitment, the process consists of just four simple steps. As you go through these steps, the main work you'll be doing will be to accumulate more of the positive emotions you will be feeling in the days, weeks, or months after you have achieved your goal.

> To accumulate emotions, all you need to do is repeat your selected emotions. As you do this, work to feel them deeply. You can cycle through them quickly, or you can sit with each emotion for a minute or more.

> Choose whichever method works best for you. The goal is to repeat your chosen emotions enough times to move you through each of the four steps in the process. This will make accumulating these emotions fun and not too arduous.
>
> Make this a habit. Set aside some time each morning or evening (fifteen minutes, thirty minutes … whatever feels right) to accumulate emotions. By making this part of your daily routine, you'll experience steady progress. Once you reach step four, you will keep accumulating these same emotions. This will increase your power and your happiness while working on your goal.

Before we dive into the specifics of how to complete the four steps, here is a quick overview of the process:

1. You will first accumulate enough emotions to begin to *believe* that you can succeed.
2. As you accumulate more of these warm emotions, you will *convince yourself* that you can succeed.
3. Then, as you accumulate even more of these same emotions, you will eliminate enough false ideas to the point that you'll *know* you will succeed. At this point, you will also start to receive assistance from your incredible mind, your higher power, and others around you. From this point on, you will be happier because you will now know that you will achieve your goal.
4. Finally, once you know you have all of this assistance, you will *become obsessed* with succeeding at

your goal. Knowing that you will succeed, it will become easy for you to do whatever it will take, and you will continue receiving even more assistance. Your results will improve, but even more importantly, you will be happier and will enjoy the process as you move forward. Your false ideas will have been replaced with truth, and you can now do anything you have the talent and ability to do.

Actions trigger feelings, and I felt this firsthand when I discovered BBE by sitting in the Porsche I dreamed of one day owning. Each time I touched the steering wheel of my Volkswagen Beetle, I felt how it would feel to touch the steering wheel of my very own Porsche. When I imagined myself sitting in the Porsche, I was in a different place doing something different. Ever since then, whenever I've set a goal, I have connected to the process of accumulating emotions by using a tactile cue with my hands. For example, I have pinched my BBE sheet (see the end of this chapter for an example), pinched a congratulatory note, or pinched something else that signified success, or I've lightly clenched my fists. I have done this over and over to train myself. Whenever I use these tactile cues, I feel all the emotions I will be feeling after I have achieved my objective.

I also incorporated a tactile cue when I was helping the University of Utah football team in 1984 by teaching them to use BBE. Their season was already underway and their coach, Chuck Stobart, saw that BBE would help the team, so he took a chance and asked me to talk to his players and teach them how to use this tool. I asked them to visualize what they would be doing in the few days after they had achieved their goal.

The team decided they'd imagine themselves eating a celebratory dinner together. I then asked them to feel how they will be feeling at that dinner. To help them connect with those emotions, I had the idea to ask each player to carry the handle of a dinner knife in their pocket. (I did not want to give them sharp knives, so I went to a restaurant supply house and bought a hundred knives, and then I went to a knife sharpening shop and had them cut off the blades and smooth the ends of the remaining handles. The knife handles were now small enough to fit in a pocket.) By using BBE and connecting with their tactile cue, the team improved, and they were all happier in the process (even though they came short of their goal). For years afterward, whenever I would meet one of the players from that team, they would tell me that they still had that knife handle and were still using it to help them move forward in their lives.

You can increase the effectiveness of BBE by using a similar tactile cue to bring up the emotions you'd like to access and more deeply attune to the power of BBE. The more you do this small action, the more you will create the positive emotions, and the more you will be able to do what you need to do. This is your path to success.

BELIEVING BY EMOTIONS

Now, it's time to fill out your own BBE sheet. Use the blank sheet at the end of this chapter as a template, and refer to the sample sheet as an example. (You'll also find additional blank BBE sheets at the end of the book.)

On a sheet of paper, your phone, or a computer, write down these items:

- Your goal and completion date (give yourself a reasonable amount of time to accomplish this; for your first goal, it should be something you can accomplish within a few days or weeks)
- The tactile cue you will use to connect with the new emotions (I suggest pinching your BBE sheet)
- Two or three benefits you—and others in your life—will gain by reaching your goal
- Three or four emotions you will be feeling in the days, weeks, or months after you have reached your goal

Once you've completed your BBE sheet, it's time to go over the four steps of BBE in detail so you can follow them as you work toward achieving your first goal.

Step One

First, you will accumulate enough emotions to initially flip the scale. This will cause you to feel a positive change, and you will now *believe* you can succeed at your goal. But this does not yet eliminate your false ideas; that will happen during the next steps.

After this initial flip, you will just keep accumulating emotions. So, if you miss this initial feeling, it is not important. But I believe you will feel a little different and a little better as the scale is flipped.

To complete step one, slowly read your entire BBE sheet. Simply reading the words and concentrating on each of the emotions you have written will begin to accumulate emotions. If you feel even a small change, you know that the tool is working.

We are all different, but my experience tells me that going through the BBE sheet four or five times will be enough for you to obtain this different feeling. A bigger goal may take more repetitions.

If you are not sure whether you have reached that feeling, just keep repeating your emotions to yourself and accumulating those same emotions. The moment will arrive, and you will know it when you feel it. You will begin to see yourself as the winner you really are.

Step Two

In this step, as you continue to accumulate emotions, you will become *convinced* that you can succeed. You will also begin to eliminate your false ideas. By this step, you will be creating in your heart a version of who you will be *after* you have succeeded. The further you move along the path of creating this new version of yourself, the more false ideas you will expose and eliminate—and the happier you will feel. All this will be happening before you do any physical work toward reaching your goal.

BELIEVING BY EMOTIONS

To complete step two, read your BBE sheet again. But, when you get to the benefits, read the first one. Then, reread each emotion. Do the same with each benefit. Each time you read an emotion, attempt to experience it more deeply.

In addition, each time you read a benefit, visualize how it will feel to have more of that benefit in your life. The more you connect your emotions to the benefits you and others will be receiving after you've reached your goal, the faster and easier it will be to accumulate emotions.

The feeling you are attempting to experience is a good, pleasant feeling. A feeling of increased confidence. A happier feeling of being your successful self.

While you're working on step two, you might find it helpful to listen to certain types of music that can change the way you feel. (Being dyslexic, I could not listen to music while I studied, and music does not help me accumulate emotions. But we are all different.) Music helps many accumulate emotions more rapidly. It can change the way you feel and can open your heart.

When you are working on a large goal, or if you are struggling to accumulate emotions, you may also find it helpful to ask your higher power for help in creating this new version of yourself. If you continue to struggle, just keep asking and accumulating emotions.

You can also sit in one spot during step one and then move to another spot when completing step two; this signals to your brain that you are shifting the way you're thinking. It will remind you that the emotions you are feeling are the ones you will be feeling after you have achieved your goal. I felt this deeply when I first sat in that Porsche.

Step Three

In this third step, as you continue to accumulate emotions, you will eliminate enough false ideas to the point that you will *know* that you will succeed. On large goals, this will take time and dedication. But the minutes and hours spent doing this will save you months, weeks, and even years in the future.

Once you have accumulated enough emotions to know that you will succeed, you will begin to receive assistance from your mind, your higher power, and others around you. I know when I am to this point because I am sure I will succeed, but I am not sure how I will make it happen. Soon after, new ideas start coming to my mind, as well as help from many sources. But the biggest benefit at this step is that knowing I will succeed brings me such an increase in happiness.

To complete step three, continue repeating the process in step two until you feel differently. This will indicate that you are beginning to see and feel the real you. You will likely feel good inside, or a little better, more pleasant, noticeably happier, more confident, or more energetic.

(In my experience, this is the step that has been most difficult because it is at this point when I briefly feel some doubt. To help me push through, I remind myself that I will soon have assistance from my incredible mind, my higher power, and other sources to help me succeed. This tool gains its real impact from our higher power. Achieving step three opens the door for us to receive the help of that power. Looking forward to this help keeps me motivated to accumulate emotions. In addition, I know that my false ideas are making their last stand and are about to be eliminated. I am about to gain an enormous level of truth about myself. With these thoughts in mind, I keep accumulating emotions and eventually reach step four.)

Realizing that you will be receiving enough help to make succeeding possible will keep you motivated to continue accumulating emotions. At this step, you are in a gold mine, not far from a vein of gold. You need to just keep drilling until you hit the gold. With this in mind, just keep accumulating emotions.

Step Four

Then, after you have accumulated even more emotions and have remained open to receiving support from your mind, your higher power, and other sources, your energy and enthusiasm will increase to the point where many ideas will come to you about how to succeed. You will be filled with happiness and confidence. In time, you may even become *obsessed* with achieving your goal, and you will fully enjoy the journey forward. It will be only a matter of time until you succeed. Knowing this, you will be able to easily do whatever it takes to succeed.

To complete step four, you will need to do three things. First, you'll need to start doing the work—and keep doing whatever it takes—until you achieve your goal. Succeeding will still require doing all the work, but now it will be fun and worth the effort. Second, you will need to continue accumulating emotions and gaining more truth to reinforce this modified view of yourself. This will remove additional false ideas, help maintain your confidence, and allow you to keep learning how to better succeed and have the courage to keep moving forward. Third, you will need to just relax and enjoy the journey. With your incredible mind, your higher power, and the world around you assisting your efforts, your success is guaranteed. If, by chance, you do not succeed, it simply means that your higher power has something even better in store for you. This has happened to me a couple of times, and every time, I've gained enough truth to succeed at something even better. This is such a happy way to live.

In the beginning—and even after you become effective at using BBE—it may not be clear when you have moved from one step to the next. That is just fine. You'll just need to keep accumulating emotions during all four steps and during your entire journey toward your goal. The most significant change you will notice in every goal you work toward will be how happy you are during the journey. That has been the number one benefit for me and others who are successfully using BBE.

BELIEVING BY EMOTIONS

Give It Time

After you take the time to listen to "The Strangest Secret," set your first goal, and accumulate enough emotions to be confident of your future success, you still have more work to do. But it will be fun and pleasant work, especially once you understand the learning curve of BBE.

When you first start using BBE, you may find that your progress feels slow or flat. This is because it will take time for you to process the emotions you are accumulating and remove the false ideas that have been controlling you. The most difficult part of using BBE is having faith in the process and just continuing to accumulate more units of emotions. As you continue to use BBE, you will expand your understanding of the tool and your ability to use it. At the same time, you will also expand your understanding of your potential. Be patient with yourself. You will succeed. It will be worth the effort.

At times, it will seem like nothing is happening; but, if you keep doing it a little longer, and then even a little longer, it will happen. These are natural laws, and they will always work. It takes time to know you will succeed. It takes time to see yourself differently. It takes time to realize how truly happy you are feeling. But the extra minutes (and even hours) spent will save you days, weeks, and months in the future.

As you continue the process, something miraculous will happen: Once you see yourself as a success, you will start thinking and acting like a successful person; you'll acquire new skills, and you'll further develop some of your inborn talents and abilities. Remember, we are wired to act in harmony with the way we see ourselves, and so once you see yourself differently, you will act differently and will produce better results; and, most importantly, you will be happier along way. You will also make some mistakes during this time—and that's okay. This is the perfect time to make mistakes, because the risk is low, and you can learn from those mistakes (see chapter 5) without creating enormous damage.

Be patient with yourself during this time. Eventually, as you keep using BBE, you will grow faster, and your rate of success will skyrocket, as shown in the chart below. Your happiness will also increase as a result. Reminding yourself of this visual can help you to enjoy the process of accumulating emotions.

In this learning curve, your first goal will occur within the first part of the line. Most of your success will come *after* you have achieved that first goal. So, for now, set an attainable, reasonable goal you know you can achieve. (At the beginning, you may also need to force yourself to move past the false ideas that are telling you not to use BBE or that BBE will not work for you.) Keep in mind that, even with a small and achievable goal, you will go through that initial period of lower production and accomplishment. Eventually, with the lies and false ideas gone, you will succeed far beyond your initial expectations; it will just take some time to do it.

One goal you might want to start with is to use BBE to remove your false ideas and gain more truth around the fact that your higher power is all-knowing and comprehends more than your finite mind can. This may be an easy goal to begin with because it will help you gain information and will require no immediate change on your part. It will also help you to be happier and will increase your faith. Your higher power loves you and wants the best for you. Remembering this will help you continue to be happy and at peace as you work toward your next goal, and then next, and so on.

Everything we do is a process, and BBE is no exception. We are always more successful when we prepare before we act, so it is necessary that you remain diligent with accumulating emotions and give the process time to unfold in the proper order.

When learning to drive we first become a good driver and then we drive fast, after we've developed our skill through practice. If we were to drive fast before becoming a good driver, the probability of an accident would be very high. Similarly, when one is learning to play a musical instrument, it is important to learn to play before giving any type of performance. If one were to try to perform before they had learned to play the instrument, it would not turn out well. The same is true in sports. Those who play in teams take time to prepare so they will not let down their other team members. They do not go on the field until they have taken many necessary steps to prepare. In all things in life, we need to take the steps in their proper order.

This is a big reason traditional growth is such a slow, hard, and frustrating process—because, in these methods, we attempt to move forward without taking the time to first remove the false ideas, gain more truth about ourselves, and change the way we see ourselves; we're not proceeding in the correct order. We are struggling rather than being filled with increased happiness during the journey.

Instead, with BBE, we first remove our false ideas, gain the necessary truth about ourselves, and change the way we see ourselves; this process creates a foundation for the exponential growth you saw in the graph. And the journey itself is easier, happier, and shorter!

Decisions, Decisions ...

BBE can also be a great help in making decisions by enabling you to feel how you will feel in the days *after* you have made the correct decision. Once you have

BELIEVING BY EMOTIONS

accumulated enough positive emotions toward a goal, your thinking will become clearer and the decision will present itself to you.

Before I discovered BBE, I had trouble making decisions. It got so bad at one time in my life that I worked out a system I thought would help me make decisions better and faster. In each case, I just asked myself what decision one particular friend (who was an attorney and was very bright) would make. I would figure out what decision he would make, and then I would make that decision. I had such a low opinion of myself and believed that I could not make a good decision, but if I thought about what a good decision-maker would do, I knew the answer.

This turned out to be a broken system because I actually had the ability all along; I just lacked the confidence to trust myself. So I trusted what I thought my friend would decide. I was just tricking myself into making good, rapid decisions.

Once I started using BBE to see myself as a successful person, I was able to think and act like a successful person—and this alone enabled me to make good decisions on my own. I still made some mistakes, but I have learned that each mistake we make gives us an opportunity to learn a lesson that will help us be even more successful in the future. The more I used BBE in the different areas of my life, the sooner I became a person who was able to rapidly make great decisions on my own.

A Few More Tips

As you continue to move forward, it might be helpful to make note of the false ideas that are eliminated. Many we do not notice, and they just fade away; but some we do notice as they are eliminated.

I still remember when I eliminated a major false idea as I was first discovering BBE. About the time when I was coming to believe I would succeed, I was sitting in my car waiting for the light to change. Then, a thought suddenly popped up in my mind that told me I could never be successful.

My mind then flashed back to being with my father when I was about ten years old. My father often took me to the farmers market. While we were there, he would point to someone and say, "He's rich, and he's a crook." We trust what our parents teach us, and I'd heard this enough times from my father that I accepted it as the truth. My young mind falsely concluded that, in order to be rich, I would have to be a crook. Years later, while sitting at that red light, I knew I had no chance to succeed because I was committed to integrity.

But I had initially flipped the scale by that point, and my mind was now helping me. It brought up memories of successful people who I knew were honest. At that moment, I recognized that my idea about needing to be dishonest to succeed was false, and I let go of it. It died as soon as I stopped believing in it.

You may also need to relisten to "The Strangest Secret" two or three times throughout the process. Earl

BELIEVING BY EMOTIONS

Nightingale's guidance can be a powerful reminder that you have the power to change your life by changing the way you think. BBE then takes this idea a step further by teaching you to use your emotions to change the way you see yourself before you begin your journey. Every little thing you do to help yourself access more positive emotions will increase your chances of success.

Finally, as you follow the four steps of BBE, remember to stay connected with your higher power and the world around you. Accumulating emotions through BBE will bring you to your truth, and as you gain more truth about yourself, your mind will gain new ideas and open you up to your higher power's guidance and new opportunities from others in your life. We are all connected, and people will come to help you succeed. The more you try to help others in the process, the faster the additional truth you need will seem to come to you. And the more you focus on lifting and assisting others, the more truth you will gain to help you succeed.

Your next step is to continue to use BBE. It will make every other thing you do much easier. But it will not remove problems; they are there to help you learn lessons and grow. Instead of weighing you down, your problems, setbacks, and even failures will become ways to learn new truths that will bring you more happiness and more success in the future. Your problems will all be easier to deal with by the time you have finished this book. You will learn to view them as your friends that will help you be stronger, develop your talents, and learn new skills. The key to all of this is to keep accumulating emotions and gaining more truth.

There is a successful version of each of us. While we are accumulating emotions, we are reconnecting with this successful version of ourselves that is gently pulling us toward our goal.

Blank BBE Sheet

My Goal:

_____

_____

Completion Date:

_____

Tactile Cue:

_____

> **REMEMBER ...**
> By continuing to accumulate more emotions, I am continuing to get a better view of my true self—and that person is gently pulling me forward.

BENEFITS:

1.

2.

3.

EMOTIONS:

1.

2.

3.

4.

Sample BBE Sheet

My Goal:

_____

Completion Date:

_____

Tactile Cue: Pinching this BBE sheet

_____

> **REMEMBER ...**
> By continuing to accumulate more emotions, I am continuing to get a better view of my true self—and that person is gently pulling me forward.

BENEFITS:

1. _____
2. _____
3. _____

Choose two or three of the following benefits, or others that are important to you:
- Learn to better use the natural laws of BBE.
- Gain more truth.
- Gain more help from my incredible mind.
- Gain more help from my higher power.
- Gain more help from the world around me.
- Learn to see myself as a winner.
- Become more of who I have the potential to be.
- Gain more control in my life.

- Find more happiness in my life.
- Gain a greater level of peace in my life.
- Become more financially secure.
- Do something I need to do.
- Change something I want to change.
- Increase my faith in my higher power.
- Increase my faith in myself.
- Become a better person.
- Have more fun being who I am.
- Be more at peace with who I am.
- Find happiness and satisfaction in the journey.

EMOTIONS:

1. _____
2. _____
3. _____
4. _____

Choose three or four of the following emotions, or others that are meaningful to you:
- Gratitude
- Excitement
- Happiness
- Pride
- Confidence
- Satisfaction
- Peace
- Love
- Joy

FIVE

Ideas That Will Help You Succeed

FIRST, I WANT TO CONGRATULATE you on what you have accomplished by reading this many pages in the book. In doing this, you have learned how to be happier in your journey going forward. This is something many successful (and many unsuccessful) people do not know. You now have a tool that will enable you to do this going forward. This tool will also help you increase your faith and your ability to follow your higher power. Congratulations.

Now, as you begin to use Believing by Emotions toward your goal, the following ideas will be helpful to you. (If you are still deciding on what goal you'd like to achieve, you can come back to this chapter and work on developing these habits and skills later.)

Thinking and Acting Like A Successful Person

Now that you have been introduced to BBE, I would like to introduce you to another skill. Used together, they will almost guarantee your success. But, far more importantly, they will guarantee you a happier, more peaceful journey on your way to success.

Successful people have developed the habit of finding a way to use everything that is happening to them as tools to help them become even more successful. This is why successful people do not quit, do not blame others or circumstances, and keep moving forward until they succeed. They are not bothered by mistakes, setbacks, failures, and difficult circumstances. They always end up learning lessons and eventually finding a way to succeed. They see these types of situations as friends placed along their path to help them learn valuable lessons.

Based on my own personal experience, going through the process of using BBE is helpful in forming the habit of thinking and acting like a successful person. When I first learned this habit, I had not yet used BBE. I'd acquired this habit as a separate undertaking, and it took me over six months to do. Now that I understand BBE better, I am suggesting you use a different approach.

With everything you've learned so far about BBE, you know that you are already a successful person. You just have some false ideas that are keeping you from seeing that fact. (Even if you have already used BBE and removed some of your false ideas, you still have many more that are holding you back.) When things go wrong, or when you are faced with a problem, take a moment to pause and remember that this experience is there for a reason. It is there to help you learn something that will help you be even more successful in the future. It may be to help you learn a new important lesson you need to learn, or it may be there to help you remove some false ideas that are keeping you from seeing that you are already a successful person.

BBE gives you a tool to rapidly learn these lessons. You do not need to fight through your false ideas to succeed. You can use BBE to accumulate enough units of emotions to gain the additional truth you need. For years, I have heard people say, "When the going gets tough, the tough get going." After discovering the power of BBE, I would now say, "When the going gets tough, it is time to stop, accumulate emotions, and remove the false ideas that are making the going so tough."

When you have a setback, just pause and say, "That is great," then find a way to learn something that will help you be even more successful in the future. Use BBE and feel how you will feel in the weeks or months *after* you have learned this lesson that your life is trying to teach you. As you do this, you will change the way you see yourself. Now your mind and your higher power are free to help you gain new skills, improve your abilities, and refine your talents. Then, achieving your goal will be easier and faster, and the journey will be more fun and joyful.

Successful people are optimistic and happy. They are able to accomplish goals which initially seemed impossible. Once I began to see everything that was happening in my life as friends, there to help me learn lessons, my life was not only happier but also incredibly easier and more rewarding. The more this habit becomes a part of your life, the easier and more fun your life will become.

I have also learned to recognize the messages from my mind in the same way. Feelings of sadness, despair, frustration, or discouragement are there to help me. They cause me to pause, slow down, and look more closely at what is actually going on. They are my friends. As I treat these feelings as friends and love them, they help me to learn important lessons. And if I keep accumulating emotions, I will move past them and will become a much better and happier person. We are all here to succeed and move forward; BBE just makes it easier, faster, and more enjoyable.

BBE can also help you learn the lessons your body is sharing with you. For example, if you lack the motivation to accomplish something that is in your best interest, you can use BBE to gain additional truth and know that you were born successful enough to succeed and achieve your objective. This will increase your desire to act and move forward.

Forming these habits of thinking and acting like a successful person will help BBE become your default action to overcome unpleasant experiences. It will help you use those experiences as stepping stones toward your greater success.

My mentor was one of the smartest men I have ever known. Before retiring, he had been the head of the Federal Housing Administration, which meant he had been in charge of about 300,000 government employees. He often told me, "Take the time to contemplate, and when the inspiration comes, have the courage to act." When I would go to him with the business challenges I was facing, he would always give me the same advice: "See it through." On a regular basis, he also reminded me of these two methods for success: First, survey large fields and cultivate small crops. And second, plan, simplify, and be strong. I always followed his advice, and it always seemed to work out. The more I applied these ideas, the easier it was for me to succeed. With the help of my higher power and BBE, I have always found a way to learn lessons from the problems I've faced.

I also have a good friend who is very successful. Like me, he has learned that, in business and in life, things are seldom smooth. He feels that the way to succeed is by learning to deal with our problems and finding successful ways to solve them.

These are two examples of people in my life who have taught me to think and act like successful people think and act. The more I do this in all areas of my life, the better things work out. When I cannot solve a problem, the very first thing I do now is pause and relax a little. Then, I use a combination of BBE, contemplation, and thinking like a successful person to move forward.

Testimonial

"Meeting Bob Raybould, and using Believing by Emotions, has changed my life. I grew up on a ranch in rural New Mexico, and I eventually found my way to the University of Utah. At nineteen years old, I started working at Apple, and I was failing at balancing my job with my computer science studies. After undergoing a major jaw surgery, I faced more challenges but managed to secure a permanent part-time role at Apple. However, things took a downturn when I lost that job temporarily and struggled with my studies, leading my parents to suggest that I return to New Mexico. Fortunately, I got my job back and managed to complete my first year of studies while also completing an internship.

"One day, while working at Apple, I met Bob Raybould, who introduced me to 'The Strangest Secret' and BBE, which he said could help me achieve any goal. Initially skeptical, I eventually embraced Bob's advice and started setting goals, including securing an internship with Boston Consulting Group.

"Though I faced rejections, including one from Apple for an engineering internship, I kept pushing forward. Bob's guidance helped me change my mindset, leading me to land an internship with Lockheed Martin, and a year later, a position with Boston Consulting Group.

> "Through Bob's mentorship, I have learned to view myself differently and pursue my goals with renewed confidence. Bob opened my eyes to my potential, helping me transform from feeling lost to achieving goals I had once thought were impossible. His teachings have been instrumental in shaping my journey and driving me toward a successful future. If *I* can do it, I can only imagine what someone else could accomplish, because I am an average person who now knows about the tool."
>
> —Ezekiel Jaramillo

Using BBE in the Face of Tragedy

Even after you've developed the ability to welcome life's challenges as lessons and opportunities for growth, you may still find yourself faced with especially difficult situations that feel insurmountable. When tragedy strikes (the loss of a loved one, a tough medical diagnosis, divorce, job loss, etc.), you may feel like you can never be happy again. But using BBE during these times can help you regain balance.

In times of tragedy and personal loss, we intellectually know that in the future we will again see things more accurately and see that we have many things to be grateful for. We know our problems will eventually be resolved, but the majority of our feelings in the moment are telling us the opposite.

In those dark times, everything can seem hopeless. When all seems lost, BBE can help us accumulate enough emotions to move us forward to our truth, to a place of happiness and well-being. It can help us see ourselves as the person we will become in the weeks and months after we are through our difficult situation. Gratitude is a key emotion for doing this.

However, while we will move through the same four steps of BBE, in cases like this, we also need to mourn our loss. If we just stuff those negative emotions and push past them, they cannot be exposed and eliminated. Very often, they need to be experienced. Depending on your situation, you may want to get outside help from a therapist to guide you through the mourning process while also using BBE to support your efforts.

When faced with tragedy, also remember that your higher power loves you, has all power and knowledge, and wants the best for you. So even when things appear to be terrible, many times, they will turn out better than you could have ever expected. You have to work to remember this, and you can use BBE to help you feel how you will feel after the mourning has been completed and you have moved forward to find the new life you've been promised.

A Method for Accumulating Emotions More Rapidly

In 1985, I had the privilege of working with Keith Henschen, PhD, who was on the staff of the University of Utah as their sports psychologist. Keith had helped the university's gymnastics team win their first NCAA championship, and many more thereafter. He was also a sports psychologist for the Utah Jazz. After discussing

IDEAS THAT WILL HELP YOU SUCCEED

BBE with Keith, he felt that I was introducing a new type of visualization.

Keith believed that there were two skills which were fundamental to effective visualization. The first skill was that of concentration. The second skill was the capacity to rapidly move from one level of being and into our zone of high performance (the "zone").

To master the skill of concentration, he had his athletes look at a coin or their thumbnail and see how long they could concentrate on it without looking away. For those who did concentrate, they immediately and easily fought through their tension and "locked in." This took them less than a couple of seconds.

Most others could only maintain their concentration for about five or six seconds before losing focus and looking away. Keith pointed out that emotional tension was forcing them to lose their concentration. He had them try again and just fight through the emotional tension until they locked in. Once they knew what they were doing, almost all could fight through that tension and lock in in less than three or four seconds. He had them repeat this, and each time, stay locked in for a longer period of time.

Next, he taught his athletes the skill of rapidly transitioning into the zone. Interestingly, he had them first learn to move themselves into a state of relaxation. They learned to do this by getting into a comfortable position and then repeating a phrase, such as, «Whole body, comfortably warm," until they felt a relaxing sensation course through their bodies. (The first time I attempted this exercise, it took me approximately thirty or forty repetitions before I felt the sensation.)

He then told them to keep practicing this exercise until they could summon that same sensation with only three or four repetitions of the words. (This took me several sessions, and in each session, it took considerably fewer repetitions to achieve the relaxed sensation.)

I am now glad that I took the time to master these skills, because they have not only helped me in the past, but they now serve to assist me in rapidly accumulating emotions with BBE.

When I transitioned into the zone for the first time, I was surprised by how much faster this exercise enabled me to accumulate emotions. As I said to myself, "Mind and body in the zone," I knew I wanted to go into the zone for accumulating emotions. After three or four repetitions of those words, I felt a change in my body. Then, as I read the emotions on my BBE sheet, or thought of the emotions, I accumulated them much more rapidly.

Mastering these two skills has an extremely broad application. They will allow you to move to an area of high performance in any area of your life, and to do so rapidly.

SIX

Using BBE to Become a Better Person

I'D NOW LIKE TO SHARE with you an example of how I used Believing by Emotions for a larger goal. A few years ago, I decided that I would use BBE for something more important than just improving my professional results. By this time, I had already learned that BBE was much more powerful than I had originally understood. So I decided to use the tool for a truly significant goal: to become a better person.

Becoming a Better Person

I knew that if I could be a better person my life would work better. I had the ability to do it, but I did not yet have the desire to change because I thought I was fine the way I was. To overcome this false idea, I planned to use BBE to gain enough truth about the benefits of becoming a better person so that I would want to make this change.

To become a better person, I set a goal to live more fully by my higher power's guidance. For me, this also meant that I would love my wife and family more, and I would be less narcissistic. (At the time, I did not think that I was narcissistic, but a therapist had told my wife that I was. I assumed I at least leaned in this direction, because I loved to be in control and loved to be right; I was very competitive and had a lot of insecurities. Having less of these qualities would help me be a better person.) In addition, at this time in my life, I was always trying to be special and stand out from other people. As I will outline in the next chapter, BBE later enabled me to move away from needing to be special and toward being a normal person with strengths and weaknesses. I am sure part of my desire at that time to be special was because I wanted to be better than others. Now, in wanting to be a better person, I wanted to love myself and others as we are. I knew that if I modified the way I saw myself, I would get more help from my mind and from my higher power to reach my goal. My completion date was eighteen months away.

BBE in Action

To help convince myself of the truth that I could become a better person, I wrote myself a letter from my wife, congratulating me on having made significant progress toward becoming a better person. I wrote it on

USING BBE TO BECOME A BETTER PERSON

a piece of notepaper and placed it in one of the accompanying envelopes. As my tactile cue, I held the note and started accumulating the emotions I would feel in the weeks and months after I became a better person.

It took me about seven days to accumulate enough emotions to convince myself that I would succeed. Once this happened, I saw myself as a better person. (I thought this was quick progress, compared to the three weeks it had taken me to reach this step when I had used BBE over fifty years earlier.)

When I began, I did not *want* to become a better person, but I knew my life would work better and I would be much happier if I made this change. I knew there were many areas of my life in which I could become better. But I did not want to change; I was content with who I was, even though I was probably stuck. I was successful, and my value was coming from my successes and material objects, and not from who I was. This created a conflict for me. Intellectually, I knew I would be better off if I were a better person. But emotionally, I did not want to do it.

This was a big moment for me in expanding my understanding of BBE. In the past, I had used the tool to believe that I could do things that my false ideas had been telling me I could not do. But this time, it was different. Now I was going to use BBE to change my desires. I did not want to become a better person, but I was going to reverse that. By using BBE, I would see myself as who I would be after I had become a better person, the complete and whole person I was when I was born. I would surround that thought with love and other warm feelings.

Flipping the scale increased my desire to become a better person. And, as I added more emotions, I solved that internal conflict. I began to feel more of the values that would come to me as I became a better person. The more emotions I added, the more I wanted to add even more emotions. Now, the successful Bob I had created was gently pulling me toward being a better person. I was on my way toward becoming a better person, and I was having fun adding emotions and enjoying a happy journey on the way to my objective.

As I continued to use BBE toward my goal, negative memories of the past came up. At first, they bothered me. But, in time, I recognized that they were just pointing out mistakes I had made when I had not treated others in a loving and kind way. These negative memories were a great learning experience and a demonstration of the value of BBE. In the past, when I had been using traditional growth to change, I would back myself into a corner, and then I would either change or I'd stay stuck in the corner. But now, by using BBE, I saw that I just needed to gain more truth concerning a better way to treat others. To do this, I needed to focus on accumulating emotions and leave the rest to the assistance I would receive from my incredible subconscious mind, my higher power, and the world around me. This pattern of feeling down before I discover more truth has been so consistent as I have

USING BBE TO BECOME A BETTER PERSON

used BBE over the years. I am now learning to rejoice whenever something is bothering me, because it means I am about to learn a valuable new truth. And long before I end up backing myself into a corner, I just accept it as a message to myself that I am ready to gain more truth and get rid of some false ideas.

With this insight, I kept accumulating emotions, and on my eighty-sixth birthday, I opened the congratulatory letter I had written. I still had a number of false ideas to overcome (as you will learn in chapter 7), but I was now feeling and acting like a better person in many ways. My original completion date had passed, and I knew I could still grow more toward becoming a better person. The false ideas stayed removed, and I continued to move forward.

Then I had a marvelous experience when I felt an incredibly powerful outpouring of love from my higher power. It was like nothing I had ever felt. The wall I had built to keep me protected from feeling and showing emotions was beginning to come down. Before, the pain of my early childhood experiences had been in charge, and I'd had no hope of ever moving beyond them. But now I suddenly found myself experiencing emotions and feeling more love in my life. I loved everyone around me. Feeling more love was wonderful, but it was a new experience, and I still had more to learn, so I used BBE to help me through this period of transition.

BELIEVING BY EMOTIONS

Enjoy the Journey

As you're using BBE to achieve your goals, remember that the end result is not so much about what you will accomplish, but about what kind of a person you will become in the process. The most important benefit you will receive from using BBE will be the happiness you'll feel during the journey and thereafter. Feeling whole, complete, content, and at peace will be the accomplishment that will bring you the most joy. Once you have flipped the scale and have continued to accumulate emotions until you know you will succeed at your goal, the barriers will start to come down. You will start finding out who you are, and you will start realizing the power of the unique talents and abilities you were born with.

And, when you have reached your goal, you will find that you'll want to continue moving forward. The successful person you have created will just keep unrelentingly pulling you onward; it will not give up on you. The false ideas that had been holding you back will again and again be exposed as false; and when you quit believing them, they will just disappear. You will finally see more and more accurately the lovable, wonderful person you were when you were born, and you will move forward and demonstrate more of who you are. Then, as you continue to move forward in one area of your life, your perception of your ability in that area will expand. You will have so much fun finding out who you have the potential to become.

Testimonial

"It's been more than two years since I first tried out Believing by Emotions, and I highly recommend it.

"In 2022, I had been wanting to clean out a few closets in my home for several years but was making very little headway. I was working with Bob at the time, and he encouraged me to try out BBE. I agreed.

"It wasn't all smooth sailing for me, though it is for many people. When I tried to accumulate positive emotions to outweigh my inertia and feelings that I would never get the job done, it was difficult for me. I'm a well of feelings, but evoking specific ones on command felt phony to me, and I was resistant. I made an effort to reduce my resistance, and I chose a physical symbol of how I would be feeling upon achieving my goal to help me. But still, I couldn't get to the strong feelings that Bob had described.

"Over time, both Bob and I concluded that each person is different, and I'm wired in a way that accessing feelings on command is a harder ask. I lowered my expectations about the strength of my feelings, and I went for less intense emotions. Over time, I was able to summon enough to get me started. Once I started, the feelings of wanting to reach my goal grew. Over the next few months, I not only decluttered my closets to a large degree (not perfectly), but I also decluttered the rest of my home. Things tended to pile up again, and I continued to use BBE to get back on track as needed.

"I liked the cleaner, fresher feelings my decluttered home gave me, and I wanted more of them. About a year later, I replaced old carpet in a few places with hardwood, and I revamped my patio. I work from home, and my brain works better when my surroundings are aesthetically pleasing to me, and BBE helped me get closer to where I want to be. (I still have goals to accomplish for my home, but some of them cost money, so I do them as I'm able to afford them.)

"I think BBE is a remarkable tool that will help anyone who is willing to try it out, and I encourage you to do exactly that."

—Sue Bergin

An Added Benefit

By using BBE to become a better person, I felt more love for others and for myself, and this helped me achieve another goal I had been struggling with: losing weight.

I've included this topic toward the end of the book because it is something you should only attempt after you have successfully used BBE for a number of other goals; at that point, you will love yourself enough to make this change in a healthy and manageable way.

Remember, we are wired to act in the way we see ourselves. I had known for many years that I should lose some weight, but because I still saw myself at my current weight, the best I could do was maintain my weight. Then, after using BBE to make progress toward becoming a better person and loving myself more, I saw myself in a new light and was able to use the tool to help me lose weight.

In the past, I had made little or no progress in this area of my life; I would lose some weight, but then I'd gain it all back. I had been using traditional growth, and my false ideas remained in place and in control. But now the approach would be very different.

Before, I had denied myself food to punish myself for overeating. There was not much joy in this. Now it was totally different. I set a goal and a completion date. I pictured myself sitting in a chair in my office, celebrating how I would be feeling for having maintained my weight loss for about six months. (Being in a different chair reminded me that this would be happening after I had succeeded at losing weight and after I had *maintained* that weight loss.) I then worked on accumulating enough emotions to believe I could succeed, convince myself I would succeed, and then come to know I would succeed. To get to this point took several hours of accumulating emotions spread over several days. I knew I had reached step four when I realized I was willing to do anything I needed to succeed. I had changed the way I saw myself; I was now seeing myself at the lower weight.

I had some setbacks, but the successful version of myself that I had created kept pulling me forward. I was doing this from early November into mid-January, during the holiday season when I would have typically gained

BELIEVING BY EMOTIONS

a few pounds. During this period, I also experienced a few family challenges. This was very enervating, and it caused me to seek some comfort food. As a result, my weight went up. But I was not bothered or discouraged. I knew I had already changed the way I saw myself, and I would soon get my energy back and my weight loss would continue.

One day, I was feeling really frustrated, and this signaled to me that I had reached a major turning point. (See step three in chapter 4.) I suddenly realized that I was feeling frustrated because I had been keeping track of how much food I'd been eating. In other words, I was acting like a dieter. When we diet, we worry about how much we are eating, and we force ourselves to eat less. On the other hand, when we use BBE, we see ourselves as the person we will be after we have lost the weight, and we love that new version of ourselves more than we love food. In the past, I would shoot myself down by feeling that I deserved a treat. This time around, I instead spent more time accumulating emotions, and I eventually came to love myself enough that it became easy to eat like a person who weighed less. From there, I just kept seeing myself as the version of myself who had reached my goal weight. Eventually, I did reach my goal, and I've been able to maintain that weight while treating my body with love.

This was a process; it did not happen overnight. Loving myself enough to take better care of my body was a step in that process. But I also needed to take the

USING BBE TO BECOME A BETTER PERSON

time to use BBE. I needed to set a goal and a completion date. I then needed to accumulate enough emotions to change the way I saw myself. Eventually, my incredible mind adjusted my actions and my metabolism to help me weigh the weight I saw myself at, because my mind was working toward harmony with my new thoughts.

For your journey, I strongly advise against using BBE to lose weight until you have had five or ten successes in other areas. We all have so many emotions connected to our sizes, shapes, and weights, so this should be one of the last goals you work on. By then, you will have more confidence in BBE and in your ability to use the tool, and you will have the self-love you'll need to help you lose weight. Every time you use BBE, you will eliminate more false ideas and gain more truth. The more truth you have, the easier it will be to use BBE, and the happier you will be.

> **Bonus Tip**
>
> Here is a helpful tip you can try after you've had some experience using BBE. When you're filling out your BBE Sheet, include a completion date for when you will reach step four (this will be different from your goal completion date). Doing this will give you a concrete time frame that will pull you forward as you move through each of the four steps.

In the next chapter, I will outline some of the additional improvements I made by using BBE. The beauty

BELIEVING BY EMOTIONS

of this tool is that we can start with small goals. And as we continue to accumulate emotions, we just keep moving forward.

SEVEN

Gaining More Peace

AS YOU'VE SEEN BY NOW, I have succeeded in using Believing by Emotions to create significant results in many areas of my life. I have used it to strengthen my faith in my higher power, improve my marriage and my relationship with my family, love myself and my body enough to easily and happily lose weight without hating and punishing myself, and increase my income to go from being bankrupt on paper at age thirty-three to being financially independent at age forty-four.

In the process of achieving these goals, BBE has allowed me to change the way I see myself. I have gone from seeing myself as someone who could not succeed to seeing myself as not only a winner but as someone who can hardly fail. In each of these moves forward, my results have far exceeded my expectations. And, by changing how I see myself, I have gained more peace than I ever imagined.

Gaining Peace

As you remove your false ideas, you will gain a better understanding of who you are. You will also gain the help of your incredible mind, and assistance from your higher power and the world around you. The combination of these forces will enable you to do things that are far beyond anything you ever thought possible, and you will find more peace within yourself and in your life.

Using BBE enabled me to finally be at peace with who I am as a person. Previously, I had spent my life feeling discontent. I was competitive and was always working to be special. I did not enjoy what I was doing, because I always wanted to find a way to do it better. This drive to be special was rooted in my early days.

I have little recollection of the details of those years, but I do remember feeling a lot of confusion, fear, and insecurity. When I was born, my father was forty years old, and my mother was just a few months shy of turning forty. None of my four grandparents were living. On the day I was born, and for a time after my birth, my father was in a veteran's hospital in Wyoming undergoing electric shock treatments for post-traumatic stress disorder, which he experienced after serving in France during World War I. For a while after his return, he did quite well, but then his war experiences caught up with him again. The treatments ultimately did not work, and he spent the remainder of his eighty-nine-year life self-medicating with alcohol.

My mother had had a difficult childhood. Her mother had died when she was just eight years old. And, a few years later, she discovered her brother deceased in their basement. He had been electrocuted by a random power surge. She did not marry until she was twenty-eight years old, which was unusual for that time. Life with my father was difficult, and to protect herself from the pain of her earlier years and the pian of living with my father, she built an emotional wall around herself that kept her from experiencing or expressing feelings.

I was born in Salt Lake City, Utah, in 1936, during the low point of the Great Depression. I imagine that having a baby in the midst of all that financial turmoil was the last thing my mother wanted. She had to return to work immediately after my birth, and I was passed around to various babysitters.

These circumstances created a big problem for me. Having parents who were emotionally unavailable left me feeling neglected. I had caregivers, but they did not care for me like parents normally should have. All of this created feelings of abandonment that went deep into my soul. This pain became a part of my experience. Rather than just accept that my parents had done the best they could, I decided that I *was not worthy of love*, and that I had deserved to be abandoned. I also must have subconsciously followed my mother's example, and to protect myself from my pain, I built a wall that would keep me from feeling or communicating my emotions. And, if anyone tried to express love for me, my wall kept me from experiencing those feelings.

Then, as I grew older, I determined that, if I became special enough, I would never again be subject to abandonment; I would never feel that level of pain again. This caused me to become very competitive, to work very hard, be judgmental, create superior results, and never let anyone get close enough to me to hurt me. This damaged my relationships, especially those with my family.

Decades later, I have been able to use BBE to let go of the need to be special, and I've come to accept myself as a normal person with my own strengths and weaknesses. By doing this, I have finally gained a sense of peace within myself, just as I am.

The Spiral

While I was using BBE to let go of my need to be special, I discovered an important element to how our false ideas keep us stuck. Imagine your journey toward growth as a spiral, where your core false idea is at the center of the spiral, with many other supporting false ideas extending outward.

In using BBE, once you reach step three and gain the help of your mind and assistance from your higher power, you are able to go directly to the center of the spiral and expose the core false idea that is holding you back. This causes your mind to eliminate that core idea. Once that core idea has been eliminated, all the supporting

GAINING MORE PEACE

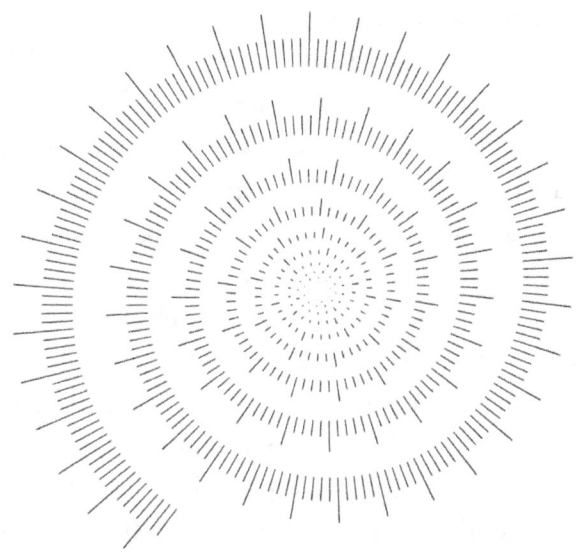

false ideas just fade away. This is one reason why you experience so much happiness when you complete step three. This is a natural law, and it's what makes BBE so powerful. The hard work is having the patience and determination to keep accumulating emotions until the core idea is eliminated.

By comparison, in most traditional approaches to personal growth, your supporting false ideas are eliminated after you have succeeded (and some are eliminated in the process of succeeding), but your core false idea remains. With that core idea still in place, you have to fight through the supporting ideas one at a time, from the outside of the spiral inward. This takes extra time and energy. If your spiral contains ten false ideas, then before

BELIEVING BY EMOTIONS

you get to the core, your success is ten times harder. In addition, in traditional growth, you sometimes go over and around your false ideas. They are not eliminated, and they come back repeatedly to slow you down.

With BBE, your lies and false ideas are permanently eliminated. This enables you to achieve your current goal and to also achieve all other future goals in that area of your life.

This is a big part of how I achieved success in business so rapidly when I used BBE, and it's why I had failed when I first tried to sell life insurance. Early on, I had so many false ideas to fight through that it wore me down, and I quit. The spiral was bigger than I could handle. But my second attempt—while using BBE—was entirely different. The truth of knowing that I would succeed eliminated my core false idea, and the remaining supporting false ideas just went away because the core was gone. It is impossible for a building to remain standing when the foundation is removed.

The same thing can happen for you. As you continue to use BBE in different areas of your life, and gain the additional truth you need to see yourself as more of the winner that you already are, you will use this additional truth to cut through the spiral and eliminate your core false idea, and the supporting false ideas will fall away as well. In this way, your path toward being at peace and content with who you are will become easier, faster, and more enjoyable.

Testimonial

"I highly recommend the concepts found within *Believing by Emotions*. My life experience suggests that we are, at our cores, emotional beings. Our emotions are part of our genetic code. For believers, I would go so far as to suggest that emotions are part of our divine design. For some reason, our Creator inserted powerful emotions into our being. We are programmed to experience emotions. We cannot escape our emotions, no matter how hard we try or attempt to fool ourselves into believing we are above them.

"Consequently, it makes sense to embrace the divine design of internally coded emotions which have been gifted to us by Someone who understands us better than we understand ourselves. Recognizing that emotions are part of our divine design gives us the confidence to harness their power for purposes of self-improvement and much-needed change.

"I have absolutely no doubt that God wants us to improve, mature, grow, develop, and blossom. I also have no doubt that our emotions can be, if properly utilized, a powerful catalyst for becoming much better human beings.

"*Believing by Emotions* is a road map to help us tap into the divinely designed benefits that are a natural product of our positive emotions. If we cannot escape our emotions, then we should reprogram them in such a way as to improve our daily habits, instill divine confidence, and draw us closer to God. *Believing by Emotions* will instruct you how to go about that process."

—Dave Ference

Uncovering Hidden False Ideas

Sometimes, our core false ideas are hidden, and we need outside help to see them before we can use BBE to eliminate them.

While I was working on letting go of my need to be special, my family was smart enough to suggest that I spend time seeing a therapist. I had been drafting this book for about three years, and my family could see that I was stuck. Luckily, I found an excellent therapist, and I spent about three hours a week with him.

During those six-plus months, he helped me see that I had a number of hidden false ideas, some of which had begun near the time of my birth. And my core false idea about needing to be special had become so strong that it had kept me from even seeing that I had these other false ideas. I had a problem, but I did not know I had a problem. I was not moving forward, and I did not know why, until I got outside help from my therapist.

Most of our false ideas are not known to us. Remember, the great majority of them have been passed on to use by others. They have come from our ancestors, those with whom we associate, and their ancestors. We do not know where they came from, when they arrived, how we got them, and where they are hidden. But it does not matter; we just need to accumulate enough emotions to

GAINING MORE PEACE

expose them. Once exposed, they are eliminated. And when we eliminate them through BBE, we do not even know when they are gone. We only know that we are much happier and that our lives are working much better. That is our biggest evidence that there were hidden false ideas that have been eliminated.

This X-ray demonstrates a famous story that can help you understand the impact of our hidden false ideas.

In 1995, a British construction worker stepped on a six-inch nail which had been protruding upward out of a plank of wood. The nail pierced the bottom of his boot and continued, unabated, in its upward direction directly

125

under the ball of his foot, slicing through the leather and exiting out of the top of his boot. The construction worker, writhing in intense pain, was rushed to a local hospital for immediate treatment. The pain was so intense that he was prescribed fentanyl, a very strong opioid painkiller, and midazolam, a sedative.

The medical team carefully removed his boot to treat the injury. To their surprise, they found that the nail had pierced his boot but had only lodged between his toes. It had not pierced his skin. The construction worker's boot had been damaged by the nail, but his foot was entirely unscathed.

This story illustrates a deep concept that applies to all of us: we may be living a lie, and we may be suffering the painful results of that lie.

Just like the construction worker who was in agony from an imagined injury, we have all, at some point in our lives, stepped on a metaphorical nail (our hidden false ideas) which has remained lodged in our boot. The pain from those false ideas takes control of our lives and holds us back. We do not remove the nail. Instead, we cut the plank of wood to match the size of our boot, and we relearn to walk with the boot permanently attached to the plank.

But it doesn't have to be this way. This is one of the great beauties of BBE. We do not need to know what our hidden false ideas are. But we do need to know where we could do better in our lives. With BBE, we set a goal and a completion date. Then, we just accumulate emotions.

As we accumulate enough emotions, we will almost magically identify and expose the false ideas that had been holding us back—even the ones that we couldn't see or will never see. Once our false ideas are exposed, our minds let them go and they simply fade away. False ideas only exist for us as long as we believe in them.

Sometimes, the hidden lie is so big that we need to get outside help. That was my situation with the false ideas I had accumulated near the time of my birth. I needed a therapist to help me see that I had a nail in my boot. I was not even aware that it was there. I had cut the plank to be the size of my foot, and I had walked on it for over eighty years. I was so used to having this false idea with me that it had become part of who I was. I needed outside help to take off the boot and see that I was just fine, that I didn't need to be special to protect myself from abandonment. Once I could get the boot off and see the truth about my whole and complete self, I could go forward and find peace.

Testimonial

"Before discovering Believing by Emotions, I was constantly chasing goals, always striving, but never feeling truly at ease during the journey of reaching them. My mind would feel anxious, and I would question when—or if—I would reach my destination. But once I started using BBE every day, something incredible happened: my mindset shifted. I stopped obsessing over 'how' and 'when,' and started feeling the emotions of already having achieved my goal.

"Practicing those emotions daily created a deep sense of peace. Anxiety faded because I knew I was going to get there. I no longer felt like I was pushing against obstacles; instead, I was flowing toward success with clarity and confidence. This process didn't just change the way I approached my goals; it transformed the way I live. Now, I experience joy in the journey, knowing that everything I desire is already unfolding as I use the tool.

"BBE is more than a tool; it's a shift in how you experience life. If you've ever felt stuck, overwhelmed, or unsure of your path, this is the missing piece. It makes success inevitable—and enjoyable."

—Lyda Mclallen

Being Human

As the therapist helped me identify my hidden false ideas, I was given the chance to use BBE to eliminate them. I set a goal to let go of needing to be special and move toward being human, with my own set of strengths and weaknesses.

First, my therapist would point out a hidden false idea. For example, I had believed that, if I ever stopped working at being special, the truth about me would be revealed. People would discover that I am not special, and I would again be abandoned. That was not true, but it was the fear that had been driving me. As long as that belief was in charge, I was forced to live in fear.

Then, together, we would uncover how I had protected myself from the pain of my early experiences. To get past the false ideas I had hidden, I had to be willing to first face the pain.

Prior to about age five, I had only one childhood memory. I can remember when we were on vacation in Oregon. I was cracking walnuts with a hammer when I hit my thumb with the hammer. I started to cry. My mother told me to think of a good thought and stop crying. My grandmother had been a Christian Science practitioner, and although my mother had not joined that faith, she used its principles to block out pain. As I grew older, I had built a similar wall to protect myself from pain.

Now, eighty years later, I was being told that I had to finish taking down that wall and reexperience all the pain of my past if I were to move forward. Before I could do this, I needed to move away from my need to be special and move toward being at peace with myself as a normal human being. I needed to take down the wall I was hiding behind and release my need to look good and perform well. I needed to really become a better human being.

I used BBE to do this, and I worked on accumulating the emotions I would feel in the weeks after I had made significant strides in this direction. In time, I had accumulated enough emotions to change the way I saw myself. Eventually, I gained more peace and freedom by seeing myself as someone who was just like everyone one else, someone with strengths and weaknesses. This gave me the courage to then take down my wall.

As I started taking down my wall, I feared that when it came down I would need to again experience the pain I had felt in my early years; the pain that had been so bad that I had to build the wall to protect myself. But I pushed on because my therapist urged me that I needed to take down my wall. And because I was using BBE, I knew that I had the assistance of my mind and my higher power, which gave me strength. To my surprise, when I took down the wall, there was nothing on the other side. There was no pain to reexperience. In its place, I found forgiveness toward my parents. My mother and father had been in a terrible situation when I was born. They had done the best they could. This whole experience allowed me to build a better experience with my parents. Both had been dead for many years, but I believe they are still alive as spirits and love me a great deal more than they could have expressed when I was young.

The spiral of false ideas I had created to support my need to be special was enormous. This ever-expanding spiral had kept me from seeing the other bigger lies that had been holding me back. If I had not had BBE (and outside help), I would have been overwhelmed. I could not have possibly lived long enough to take down those false ideas one at a time. Going step by step, from the outside of the spiral inward, would have seemed impossible. Even with the help of BBE and being able to attack the core false idea, the process still took time and effort.

Taking down my wall was only part of the process. For a while, I became stuck and was not making much progress. Then I realized I needed to set a better goal for myself. Oftentimes, when I set a goal, I have to revise it to make sure I have worded it correctly, but this time, I needed to create a totally different goal. I chose as my new goal to love my higher power and others more fully.

It took time and work to change the way I saw myself so that I could achieve this new goal. I am still working on it, and this has led me to set several other goals in this area of my life. Once again, as I experience success with each of my goals, I am much happier. My eyes are being opened concerning my potential, and I am becoming a better person.

Accomplishing this objective has brought me so much peace. My need to be special was so strong that it controlled my life. Now I am moving closer to accepting myself for who I am, just like everyone I know. I have more strengths than weaknesses, and I am learning to embrace the fact that I have weaknesses because everyone has them. Along the way, my mind and my higher power are giving me enormous help.

In "The Strangest Secret," Earl Nightingale says, "Don't compete; create." For decades, my false belief that it was good to be special kept me from following the most important half of this statement. Back then, I was *creating* great ways to make money for my clients, and I was very creative in business. But I was *competing* all the

BELIEVING BY EMOTIONS

time with everyone. I was always judging to see who was better or best. I always needed to do more and be more.

By using BBE to see myself as a normal person, with strengths and weaknesses, I was able to love others for their own unique sets of strengths and weaknesses. And this enabled me to follow the full meaning of Nightingale's statement. I began to better understand what he meant when he said, "Don't compete; create." The less we compete against others—and the more we focus instead on loving and serving others—the happier we are and the easier it is for us to love ourselves. And, in that love, we find peace.

When I was trying to compete with everyone else, I was stuck in the lie that I needed to be special. But when I accepted myself—with all of my flaws and strengths—I was able to turn my focus toward loving others and creating value for others. And, in turn, I found more peace within myself.

Using BBE to more fully love my higher power and others has helped more than anything else to move me forward as a normal human with strengths and weaknesses. We all need each other. The stronger I become, the more successful I become, the more confident and positive I become, and the more I can love, lift, and help others. The more I lose myself in serving others, the more I am able to find myself. The more I move beyond needing to be special, the more I can lift others. BBE then enables me to reduce my weaknesses and increase my strengths.

This has taken time, and it is still something that I'm working on. I used BBE to set my goal and a completion date. I went through the four steps and made some progress. But again, the greatest growth came after my completion date as my love for myself and others has continued to grow. It has been a wonderful thing to experience. I am now at peace with who I am and with my circumstances. At the same time, I know I still have many more false ideas to eliminate. But the process is now fun, and I am excited to keep doing it.

Strengthening Your Belief in Your Higher Power

Another path toward more peace is to use BBE to strengthen your belief in your higher power and improve your spiritual connection through meditation or prayer. We are all different; some of us have a harder time believing and connecting than others. You might choose to use BBE to help you see yourself as someone who has an easier time with this.

We have all acquired false ideas that tell us not to follow or listen to our higher power. For several years before I became a believer, I worked hard at finding happiness and success, but it was not working for me. Later, after I had been blessed to feel the transforming power of my higher power's spirit, I found that following my higher power was the fastest and best path to my greatest happiness and success.

Our higher power loves us as we are, but also desires that we grow and fulfill our potential. We need to love ourselves in this same way. We can use BBE to find peace in loving ourselves and others as we are, while we also grow to more fully believe in our higher power and listen to the guidance we receive. And the more faith we have, the more we can use that faith to move ourselves forward. In turn, our higher power will provide us with more assistance to make the path easier.

Remember that our ability to modify our self-view comes from the transforming power of our higher power's spirit. BBE and the changes we can make in our lives are enabled by our higher power, the source of all absolute truth. The more truth we have in our lives, the better our lives work.

Other than having a transformational experience brought to you directly from your higher power, the fastest way I know to strengthen your faith is to use BBE. If you want to believe more deeply and meditate or pray more effectively, BBE will help you modify the way you see yourself so that you can feel more of your higher power's love. It will eliminate the false ideas that are telling you not to believe in and connect with your higher power. At the same time, it will also replace those false ideas with the truth that your higher power is all-knowing, loves you, and wants the best for you.

One of my current goals is to use BBE to more fully believe that my higher power can comprehend more than I can. I know that this is an absolute truth, but I still have some false ideas that are keeping me from emotionally internalizing it. These false ideas must be there; I can feel them keeping me from a better understanding of the truth. But I do not know what they are. As I use BBE to help me with this goal, I can feel that I am moving forward as my false ideas are being removed. I see myself differently, and this causes me to think and act differently, which produces different results. I do not know what false ideas I am getting rid of; I do not need to know what they were or where they came from. They are gone and are of no interest to me. I am happier and more peaceful as I am becoming more and more convinced that my higher power can comprehend more than I can.

I hope you will consider using BBE to help you become an even more committed believer. Your higher power is real and loves you. If you want to feel more of that love, you need to first strengthen your faith. There are many ways to do this, but using BBE will make it much easier for you to do the things that will move you in that direction. And you will be so much happier along the way.

… … … … … … … **EIGHT** … … … … … …

Sharing the Bounty

MY GOAL IS TO DISTRIBUTE this book (and my other book, *Success by Emotions*) to over one million individuals during the next two years. To accomplish this very aggressive objective, I will need your help. I need champions who will help me in helping others—especially young people—improve their lives and see better results.

Now that you've reached the final chapter of this book, I'm asking you to spend the five or six hours it will take to use the principles of Believing by Emotions and create value in your own life so you can encourage others to use this tool.

I have spent more than four years creating this book so that it can benefit you and everyone else you will share it with. In that time, I have worked to understand BBE more fully so that it could help everyone, no matter what

BELIEVING BY EMOTIONS

challenges they may be facing. And the rewards I have received in the process of doing this have been great.

I need readers—like you—to invest time in themselves so they can create results in their own lives and then help others create results in their lives. You will receive great rewards as you use BBE. But those rewards will pale in comparison with the happiness you will receive as you enrich the lives of others by giving them the ability to accomplish their goals faster and easier than they ever thought possible. As it says on the book cover: *Achieve the impossible by receiving more help from your higher power.*

If you are not yet ready to use BBE, then I congratulate you on taking the time to read this book. You are now in the position to make a choice about using the tool whenever you need it. In the meantime, I ask that you share this book with others so that we can help them to also know about the power of BBE. When they are ready to use it to improve their lives, they will have it at their fingertips.

Remember, when we were born, we each had a clear view of how wonderful and great we were (and still are). Then, as life happened, we accumulated false ideas from a number of different sources. These have kept us from seeing who we really are. These false ideas are hidden from our view, like the part of an iceberg that is underwater, lurking unseen. They are held in place by our emotions, and even though we cannot see them, they are holding us back. For the most part, we intellectually know what we need to do to achieve our goals. But the false ideas we have accumulated—and the emotions that hold them in place—hold their own power and keep us from doing many of the things we want to achieve.

Believing by Emotions (BBE) is a tool that enables you to use your emotions to expose your false ideas. And, once they are exposed as false, your mind eliminates them. With them removed, you see yourself more accurately. Now your incredible mind and your higher power are free to help you achieve your objectives.

The problem you may face right now is that your emotions may be telling you not to use this tool or share this book, as I have requested. In the past, you may have learned to make decisions based on logic, not emotions. Using emotions to solve a problem may still feel counterintuitive. But using your emotions is the fastest and easiest way to gain more happiness in your life.

You may also have some false ideas that are keeping you from using BBE because you fear failure. Perhaps you have failed in the past, and you're afraid you may fail again. Whatever may be holding you back, you can turn it around and use the power of your emotions to compel you toward more happiness and success rather than keeping you stuck. And, even if you do not fully succeed in achieving your goal, you will have felt so much happiness during the journey and you will have learned valuable lessons that will help you be more successful in the future. That in itself is a significant achievement.

As we've discussed, BBE is based on the natural laws that we each have our own unique set of false ideas, and

BELIEVING BY EMOTIONS

that we can accumulate emotions to remove those false ideas and improve our lives by knowing our true selves. It is like the law of gravity; it always works. But, to allow these laws to work for you, you need to keep accumulating emotions, even when you feel like giving up, until you expose and eliminate your false ideas.

For your first attempt at using BBE, please do not set a huge goal or objective. Your first goal will be the hardest to achieve because you will be overcoming two sets of false ideas: those that are keeping you from succeeding, and those that are keeping you from using BBE. The second set of false ideas will no longer exist once you've successfully used BBE to reach your first goal, but they will be there when you're first getting started. If you're feeling stuck and need a push to keep working at accumulating emotions, I suggest that you move to a goal that is easier to accomplish. Remember, our results are the hardest and take the longest to change. The next hardest to change are our actions. But the easiest thing to change is the way we see ourselves. Once we change the way we see ourselves, we act in harmony with that self-view. We do what that person does, and those actions produce the results that we want to create. So pick one area of your life where you want to reconnect with the true potential you were born with. Once you see yourself as a success in that area of your life, it will build within you the desire to achieve other more difficult goals, and you will be starting with more faith in yourself and more faith in BBE.

SHARING THE BOUNTY

"The Strangest Secret" is one of the best outlines for traditional growth that has ever been recorded. To my knowledge, since it was first released in 1953, it has sold more copies than any other. Even though it was recorded in the middle of the last century, it still does a masterful job of helping us understand the incredible power of the human mind. But, for all of its timeless value, "The Strangest Secret" (like all methods of traditional growth) is very different from Believing by Emotions.

With this book and the tool it introduces, we are making significant changes to traditional approaches to growth. In both traditional growth and BBE, we are asked to set a goal, establish a completion date, and select something that we will be doing after we have achieved our goal. And here is where BBE sets itself apart as a revolutionary new tool. In BBE, we are not working to become the person who can achieve our goal. We are that person right now; we do not need to change anything about ourselves to succeed. Instead, we are accumulating enough emotions to first see ourselves as that person. We then believe we are already that person, and we use BBE to remove the false ideas that are keeping us from seeing the truth that we were born with all the talents and abilities we need to succeed. Once we see ourselves more accurately, we naturally do what we need to do to succeed, and we have a wonderful journey. There is no need to wait to have this much fun.

To remove those false ideas, we use emotions combined with intellectual understanding to expose these

BELIEVING BY EMOTIONS

false ideas. In both traditional growth and BBE, we intellectually believe we can achieve our goal; otherwise, we would not have chosen that goal. With traditional growth, we fight through the ideas that are holing us back. With BBE, we remove our false ideas before we begin.

In using BBE, we recognize that the emotions that are holding our false ideas in place are telling us we cannot do it (or that doing it will be difficult to achieve). Those emotions are much too strong to be removed by intellectual arguments. We need to fight fire with fire. We need to use new, positive emotions to outweigh our existing negative emotions. We need BBE.

With BBE, we accumulate enough emotions to outweigh and expose the old emotions as false. Our emotions have more power over us than our intellectual reasoning. In BBE, we recognize this, and we accumulate emotions connected with how we will feel in the days, weeks, or months after we have achieved our goal. We then continue to accumulate these emotions until we can outweigh the emotions that are holding our false ideas in place. Once these false ideas are exposed as false, our minds have no further reason to hold on to them, and these false ideas are eliminated. We now see ourselves as a person who has already successfully achieved our goal. Our minds now almost force us to act like that person. And, because we now see ourselves as having succeeded, our higher power can help us without violating our freedom to choose. We move on easily to success and we are happy through the entire journey. As we move on to success, our minds are opened, and we see that the potential we were born with far exceeds anything we had previously dreamed of. This further increases our energy, our enthusiasm, and our happiness on our journey.

All these factors motivate us to keep accumulating emotions. This is the hard part about using BBE. We need to keep accumulating emotions until we have gone through all four steps in the process. We need to accumulate enough emotions to believe we can succeed, then enough to convince ourselves that we can succeed, and then enough to know that we will succeed. When we know that we will succeed, we are willing to joyfully do whatever it takes to succeed. Our minds and our higher power are then free to help us. We will succeed, but the best part will be that we will enjoy the entire journey on the way to our success.

Whenever I reach this point in the process, I never worry about what might cause me to fail. If, by chance (and this has only rarely happened over the last fifty years), something happens to prevent me from succeeding, this is fine because the journey will have been a happy one, and I will have learned many things that will help me in the future. And, most importantly, I will know that my higher power has something even better in store for me. With the very few failures I've experienced have come even greater successes.

There is another significant difference between traditional growth and BBE. With BBE, we do not need to do the thirty-day test presented in "The Strangest Secret." Instead, we utilize the habit of thinking and acting like successful people. When we face a setback, we do not try to use the thought of success to fight through the problem. We instead pause and rejoice because we have BBE and are about to use it to learn a valuable lesson. We are already confident that we will succeed. A setback is not the end of the line; it is simply a learning experience. With this mindset, we pause and let BBE help us figure out what we can learn to be even more successful in the future. We also use BBE to feel how we will feel after we have applied this knowledge and moved on to greater success. In time, using BBE becomes our knee-jerk reaction whenever we face a setback.

Another difference between BBE and traditional growth arises when we are fighting against the pull of our emotions, particularly when we are working to not do something that will harm us, or when we are working to avoid seeking something that is not in our best interest. We intellectually know it is not the best path to follow, but our emotions and the temptations we feel are drawing us down that path. If we continue to stuff our emotions, they can grow to the point that we end up acting on them. We cannot effectively use BBE to stop doing something; instead, we can use it to help us gain more truth and move us toward what we intellectually know is in our best interest. Sometimes this is not clear. I have sometimes needed to ponder and meditate to find the best goal that will help me not only do the thing that

SHARING THE BOUNTY

is in my best interest but to use this as an opportunity to become an ever more committed believer. If I become yoked with my higher power, as two oxen are equally yoked together, my higher power will carry half the load. My yoke will be easy and my burden light. This offer is available to all of us. Whoever we are and whatever we believe, our higher power is always there, willing to step in and be yoked with us. The more we can accept this fact, the more help we can gain.

If we use BBE and choose a goal that is better for us than the one our emotions are pulling us toward, we can then accumulate enough emotions to move through the four steps—and we accomplish two objectives. First, we gain more desire to achieve the objective that is better for us. Second, we gain enough truth to clearly understand why it is the better path to go down. This eliminates the power of our previously held false ideas and the emotions that were holding them in place.

This is why BBE has been so helpful to me in losing weight. I have gained so much love for myself and my body, and so much truth as to why being healthier will benefit my life, that I have learned to love my body more than I love food. This has made eating less and losing weight so much easier.

Even when we understand all of these reasons why BBE is so unique and so powerful, we can still sometimes find ourselves feeling discouraged throughout the process. Sometimes this happens when we are tired and worn down; fatigue makes cowards of us all. When this happens, we need to take a break and come back rested. Other times, this happens when we are not willing to keep trusting in BBE. If you ever find yourself getting impatient and you want things to go according to your timetable, remember that the most important benefits of using BBE are the happiness you gain and who you will become in the process; these are much more important than whatever you are able to accomplish or how quickly you can reach your goal. Rather than worrying about how long it's taking to achieve your goal, focus instead on eliminating your false ideas and moving yourself forward; let everything else unfold as it will. You have a tool that will enable you to be happier. It will help you modify your self-view and gain the help of your mind and your higher power. This is worth being patient for. When you find you are not enjoying the journey, just pause, and accumulate emotions. That will get you back on track. And, if that does not quickly help, then you can pause to learn what you need to learn to move forward.

Also remember that your successes will build upon each other over time. Each new success will expand your understanding of your full potential. The more you use BBE, the easier it will be to achieve bigger and bigger goals. With this tool in your hands, your potential truly is limitless.

It is my sincere wish that you will start using BBE and enjoying all of the many wonderful ways it will transform your life and bring you significantly more happiness through the journey. I also hope you will soon be willing to forward this book to others, because I believe it will help them to find success and happiness in their journey forward. They may not use it immediately, but they will at least know that this tool is available to them when they need it. If anything is holding you back from doing either of these, you might consider using BBE to break through that resistance. You could set a goal to reread the book, use the tool, or share the book. Then list the benefits that will come to you and the emotions you will feel after reaching your goal. Achieving this small goal will enable you to have more happiness right now. Whichever of these goals you choose, it will bring you more happiness in your own life and more happiness in the lives of those you know.

Final Comments

CONGRATULATIONS ON REACHING THE END of this book and beginning your incredible journey with Believing by Emotions. I hope that this valuable tool will help you gain more happiness and achieve your goals more quickly and easily—and, most importantly, that it will help you find more truth and peace in all areas of your life. To receive tips on how to get even more out of BBE, I encourage you to visit https://www.believingbyemotions.com and enter your email address for regular updates.

In these early days, as you begin to use BBE, please remember that it is hard for us to do something new on our own. Finding encouragement from others can help keep you motivated to stick with the process. You will soon have more help from your incredible mind, your higher power, and the entire universe. If you need encouragement to keep going, watch some of our videos, meditate and connect with your higher power, and serve someone a little better. Tell someone what you are trying to do, so that they can give you support along the way. You can also report to them on your progress (or lack thereof). Being willing to connect and be vulnerable in this way will be freeing and very helpful. All of these things will help you keep at it.

As I mentioned earlier, in the beginning, it is better to stick with smaller, reasonable goals that intellectually make sense to you. Eventually, your successes will build your self-confidence. They will also build your trust and confidence in BBE. The improvements that you will make after achieving your first goal will far exceed your current expectations, and you will be able to achieve bigger and bigger goals each time you use BBE.

As you use BBE, you will likely discover things that I have not discussed in this book, things that will improve this book. I hope you will share them with me so that we can deepen our understanding of BBE together, and so that I can continue to revise the book for future editions. I would also like to hear your story of how you have improved your life using BBE. I will be sharing these testimonials online so that even more people can learn about the benefits of this incredible tool. To get in touch, email me at info@believingbyemotions.com

Sharing Believing by Emotions

As I mentioned in the final chapter of this book, I would like to see over one million individuals benefit

FINAL COMMENTS

from BBE and enjoy its results. If you have found value in using BBE, I ask that you help me in distributing this book by sharing it with everyone you know. Even if you are not yet ready to use the tool, I am sure you can see that it is based on sound principles. Everyone deserves to be happier and have more peace in their lives, and you can help others by sharing this book. I want everyone to just keep forwarding it so it can reach as many people as possible. You can direct people to receive a free copy at https://www.believingbyemotions.com

I want to help others use BBE to set goals, accumulate wonderful emotions, and expose and eliminate as many of their false ideas as possible and replace them with truth. I want to do the same for myself, too. As we do this together, we all move toward being more whole and complete, and our focus will be to love and be loved. When I watch my three-year-old great-grandchildren play together, I see that they are eager to help each other succeed and help each other find more happiness in their lives. That is what I hope this book will bring to the world.

We each will use BBE to accomplish different goals, and we each will remove many different false ideas. Our journeys will be different, but because we are using BBE, they will all be joyous. Knowing that this tool can help us be like little children full of love—willing to love others as they are now and willing to allow others to love as we are now—our shared objective will be to help each other move forward faster.

As I look back on everyone who has benefited from BBE over the past several decades, I feel a lot of love, appreciation, and support. I did not spend years doing research or studying to discover this tool. I simply listened to "The Strangest Secret" and then sat in a Porsche. The last five years I spent attempting to better understand BBE have improved my life in so many ways, and I am thankful for this experience. I am thankful to my higher power and acknowledge all the guidance I have received in drafting and marketing this book. I am also very thankful for those who have opened their hearts and minds enough to try BBE. And I am thankful in advance for those who will use BBE in the future. Finally, I am thankful for you, for trusting in me and in the miraculous process of Believing by Emotions.

I hope you are willing to let BBE improve your life. As I said in the beginning, it takes courage to try something new and different. But I know you have that courage within you, and the effort you put into using BBE will open up infinite potential for you. I wish you all the best for your ongoing success!

—Bob Raybould

About the Author

OVER THE COURSE OF FIVE decades as a successful salesman and businessman, Bob Raybould has utilized his self-improvement tool, Believing by Emotions (BBE), to further his career and enrich his personal life.

In 1961, when the Berlin Wall went up, Bob served in Germany as the Report of Survey officer for the entire Seventh Army. In this role, he had unlimited power to either hold or relieve offenders accused of destroying or stealing government property. This meant that he was responsible for reviewing the work of colonels and lieutenant colonels who were four or five ranks higher than him. Asking these officers to modify their reports was (in a great understatement) challenging. After serving in that role for two years, he was awarded the Seventh Army Certificate of Achievement.

BELIEVING BY EMOTIONS

A few years later, while Bob was in the early stages of financial planning, he was given a great opportunity. In 1969, a change in the tax law enabled insurance companies to buy oil fields. In the past, these companies had lent money for the purchase of oil fields, and the new tax law eliminated such transactions. Bob's friend, Vince Allen, was one of the few people to recognize this opportunity, and he asked Bob to contact life insurance companies. Working with Vince and his company, Petro Search, Bob helped Aetna Life buy the first oil field ever purchased by an insurance company.

In the mid-1980s, Bob introduced the University of Utah football team to BBE and showed their players how to use the tool to improve their performance. Later, in 2004, the team's coach, Urban Meyer, asked Bob to work with six of his players during the offseason. Four of those players went on to play in the NFL. Bob also worked with about twenty-five players during Utah's undefeated season, which was a great experience for Bob, who is a sports junkie and an avid Utah fan.

Bob again brought the principles of BBE to the sports world when he helped a Utah basketball player named Johnnie Bryant (now the associate head coach for the Cleveland Cavaliers, and former associate head coach for the New York Knicks) increase his free-throw percentage. Bryant had made 80 percent during his junior year; during his senior year, after working with Bob in the offseason and using BBE, his percentage improved to 90 percent.

ABOUT THE AUTHOR

In 1987, Bob joined John T. Sweazey to form a mortgage banking firm, TRI Financial, which filled a great need when the financial crisis of the late 1980s put most savings and loan firms out of business. In 2003, TRI sold its almost $2 billion portfolio of loans to Pittsburgh National Bank, making great returns for their investors.

In the mid-1990s, Bob helped a group of former CIA employees create a data mining firm called DTM Research Inc., which provided services for several large corporations and was capable of mining data and producing results far above what was being done commercially at the time.

In 2000, Bob helped his son and his partner launch Arlington Value Management, a very successful investment firm that outperformed the market by over 8 percent for about twenty years.

Since 2010, Bob has invested in start-ups with great potential, particularly in the health-care innovation sector. He has invested in multiple companies focused on diagnostics and therapeutics, believing that their technologies can positively impact patients and global health for decades to come. One of these companies has developed a groundbreaking technology for the early detection of cancer, identifying the disease at the earliest possible stages. Another company has introduced several disruptive technologies, including one that stops invading pathogens from reproducing, and a point-of-care molecular diagnostics platform that detects and tracks the transmission of diseases globally. Bob's investments reflect his commitment to future generations, ensuring they will benefit from advanced medical technologies and improved health-care outcomes.

Over the last five years, Bob has been working to better understand BBE so that others can use it and double their speed in moving forward and achieving their goals. This book is a result of that work.

Blank BBE Sheets

ON THE FOLLOWING PAGES, YOU will find several blank BBE sheets. As you use BBE to accumulate emotions, you will likely be inspired to revise your goal, benefits, and/or emotions as they evolve throughout the process. For this reason, you may need to create several versions of your BBE sheet for each goal.

If you find yourself running low on BBE sheets, you can also photocopy the following pages and create additional copies so you can continue to explore new goals and tap into your unlimited potential!

My BBE Sheet

My Goal:

_____

_____

Completion Date:

_____

Tactile Cue:

_____

> **REMEMBER ...**
> By continuing to accumulate more emotions, I am continuing to get a better view of my true self—and that person is gently pulling me forward.

BENEFITS:

    1.

    2.

    3.

EMOTIONS:

    1.

    2.

    3.

    4.

My BBE Sheet

My Goal:

_____

_____

Completion Date:

_____

Tactile Cue:

_____

> **REMEMBER ...**
> By continuing to accumulate more emotions, I am continuing to get a better view of my true self—and that person is gently pulling me forward.

BENEFITS:

1.

2.

3.

EMOTIONS:

1.

2.

3.

4.

My BBE Sheet

My Goal:

_____

_____

Completion Date:

_____

Tactile Cue:

_____

> **REMEMBER ...**
> By continuing to accumulate more emotions, I am continuing to get a better view of my true self—and that person is gently pulling me forward.

BENEFITS:

1.

2.

3.

EMOTIONS:

1.

2.

3.

4.

My BBE Sheet

My Goal:

_____

_____

Completion Date:

_____

Tactile Cue:

_____

> **REMEMBER ...**
> By continuing to accumulate more emotions, I am continuing to get a better view of my true self—and that person is gently pulling me forward.

BENEFITS:

    1.

    2.

    3.

EMOTIONS:

    1.

    2.

    3.

    4.

My BBE Sheet

My Goal:

_____

_____

_____

Completion Date:

_____

Tactile Cue:

_____

> **REMEMBER ...**
> By continuing to accumulate more emotions, I am continuing to get a better view of my true self—and that person is gently pulling me forward.

BENEFITS:

1.

2.

3.

EMOTIONS:

1.

2.

3.

4.

My BBE Sheet

My Goal:

_____

_____

_____

Completion Date:

_____

Tactile Cue:

_____

> **REMEMBER ...**
> By continuing to accumulate more emotions, I am continuing to get a better view of my true self—and that person is gently pulling me forward.

BENEFITS:

    1.

    2.

    3.

EMOTIONS:

    1.

    2.

    3.

    4.

My BBE Sheet

My Goal:

_____

_____

Completion Date:

_____

Tactile Cue:

_____

> **REMEMBER ...**
> By continuing to accumulate more emotions, I am continuing to get a better view of my true self—and that person is gently pulling me forward.

BENEFITS:

1.

2.

3.

EMOTIONS:

1.

2.

3.

4.

My BBE Sheet

My Goal:

_____
_____
_____

Completion Date:

_____

Tactile Cue:

_____

> **REMEMBER ...**
> By continuing to accumulate more emotions, I am continuing to get a better view of my true self—and that person is gently pulling me forward.

BENEFITS:

1.

2.

3.

EMOTIONS:

1.

2.

3.

4.

My BBE Sheet

My Goal:

_____

_____

Completion Date:

_____

Tactile Cue:

_____

> **REMEMBER ...**
> By continuing to accumulate more emotions, I am continuing to get a better view of my true self—and that person is gently pulling me forward.

BENEFITS:

1.

2.

3.

EMOTIONS:

1.

2.

3.

4.

My BBE Sheet

My Goal:

_____

_____

_____

Completion Date:

_____

Tactile Cue:

_____

> **REMEMBER ...**
> By continuing to accumulate more emotions, I am continuing to get a better view of my true self—and that person is gently pulling me forward.

BENEFITS:

1.

2.

3.

EMOTIONS:

1.

2.

3.

4.

My BBE Sheet

My Goal:

_____

_____

_____

Completion Date:

_____

Tactile Cue:

_____

> **REMEMBER …**
> By continuing to accumulate more emotions, I am continuing to get a better view of my true self—and that person is gently pulling me forward.

BENEFITS:

1.

2.

3.

EMOTIONS:

1.

2.

3.

4.

My BBE Sheet

My Goal:

_____

_____

_____

Completion Date:

_____

Tactile Cue:

_____

> **REMEMBER ...**
> By continuing to accumulate more emotions, I am continuing to get a better view of my true self—and that person is gently pulling me forward.

BENEFITS:

    1.

    2.

    3.

EMOTIONS:

    1.

    2.

    3.

    4.

My BBE Sheet

My Goal:

_____

_____

Completion Date:

_____

Tactile Cue:

_____

> **REMEMBER ...**
> By continuing to accumulate more emotions, I am continuing to get a better view of my true self—and that person is gently pulling me forward.

BENEFITS:

1.

2.

3.

EMOTIONS:

1.

2.

3.

4.

My BBE Sheet

My Goal:

_____

_____

Completion Date:

_____

Tactile Cue:

_____

> **REMEMBER ...**
> By continuing to accumulate more emotions, I am continuing to get a better view of my true self—and that person is gently pulling me forward.

BENEFITS:

1.

2.

3.

EMOTIONS:

1.

2.

3.

4.

My BBE Sheet

My Goal:

_____

_____

Completion Date:

_____

Tactile Cue:

_____

> **REMEMBER ...**
> By continuing to accumulate more emotions, I am continuing to get a better view of my true self—and that person is gently pulling me forward.

BENEFITS:

1.

2.

3.

EMOTIONS:

1.

2.

3.

4.

My BBE Sheet

My Goal:

_____

_____

_____

Completion Date:

_____

Tactile Cue:

_____

> **REMEMBER ...**
> By continuing to accumulate more emotions, I am continuing to get a better view of my true self—and that person is gently pulling me forward.

BENEFITS:

1.

2.

3.

EMOTIONS:

1.

2.

3.

4.

My BBE Sheet

My Goal:

_____

_____

_____

Completion Date:

_____

Tactile Cue:

_____

> **REMEMBER ...**
> By continuing to accumulate more emotions, I am continuing to get a better view of my true self—and that person is gently pulling me forward.

BENEFITS:

1.

2.

3.

EMOTIONS:

1.

2.

3.

4.

www.ingramcontent.com/pod-product-compliance
Lightning Source LLC
Chambersburg PA
CBHW070319010526
44107CB00004B/359